LET'S RE-IMAGINE THE WORLD TOGETHER

Soft power is the new hard edge

Mike Stevenson

DEDICATION

To my darling Mary, whose love and support has sustained me for over a decade.

To the late Sir Ken Robinson, whose talks and books resonated with me and inspired me to keep campaigning for creativity.

To Sir David Attenborough for his lifetime of promoting education on the environment as on par with the three Rs.

To all those unheralded heroes whose voluntary efforts sustain the world.

TABLE OF CONTENTS

INTRODUCTION

1	We've Got it Wrong	13
2	Greed	16
3	Damaged Our Planet	19
4	Let the Young Flourish	23
5	Chance to Put Things Right	27
6	Close the Gap	31
7	Start Nursing the Planet	34
8	Give Leadership to Young People	38
9	Human Beings	41
10	Endless Capacity	46
11	Creative & Imaginative	49
12	Anything is Possible	53
13	Everyone Has a Story	61
14	Four Primary Schools	65
15	Get a Job	75
16	The Band	81
17	Job Search	86
18	The Bullies	89
19	Cream	93
20	Our Travels	97
21	Culture Shock	101

22	A Day I Will Never Forget	104
23	London	107
24	The Streets of London	114
25	Indiscretions of Cat	120
26	Emergence of Inner Strength	126
27	Dublin Here I Come	133
28	The Troubles	136
29	Tale of Two Cities	143
30	Penniless & Weightless	149
31	Striped Pyjamas	155
32	A New Work Ethic	158
33	Cat Stevens	164
34	Part of a Bigger Picture	169
35	College Days	174
36	Now What?	180
37	Unleashing the Power of People	186
38	Oh Baby	193
39	Young Volunteer Force	196
40	Next	1
41	Job Security	1
42	I Have Learned	1

A NOTE FROM THE AUTHOR

ABOUT THE AUTHOR

ACKNOWLEDGEMENTS

A huge thanks to Linda Vettrus-Nichols for resurrecting my memoir, which had been shelved for many years.

My utmost appreciation to Simon Haigh and Ambassador Terry Earthwind Nichols whose invitation to contribute to the World Thought Leaders events, inspired me to finally publish my ideas and lifetime learnings in this book.

To Carlos Alba of *Carlos Alba Media*, whose patient early edits brought my story to life.

Thank you to my siblings Eileen, Brian, and Tony for their love and support.

A grateful thanks to Mum and Dad for their forgiveness of the years I spent off the radar.

INTRODUCTION

Soft power is the new hard edge. So, what do I mean by that? Soft power is about compassion and connection, using stories rather than stats, facts, figures, and lectures. It is the art of 21st-century leadership. The age of muscular leadership will soon give way to empathetic and persuasive leadership. That is not weakness—it is strength. Compassion is courage and a vital characteristic of leadership. You can never win people over with diktat. Anyone who has experienced leadership without vision—one that is focused on task delivery—will understand. Leadership is about learning how to communicate. If governments want people to follow their policies, they need to make them clear, purposeful, and in the public's interest.

To do so, leaders must present a vision that people can experience in their imaginations.

Martin Luther King's great 'I Have a Dream' speech focused not on the problem but on a world in which black and white people enjoyed harmonious coexistence as equals.

A city designed for people is more persuasive than a war on carbon emissions.

Legacy is more important than success and power.

"Every man for himself" and "We live in a dog-eat-dog world" will be remembered as hideous remnants of a past age.

Let's get back to the concept of seventh-generation thinking, where seventh-generation stewardship urges the 'current' generation of humans to live and work for the 'benefit' of the seventh generation into the future. I'm not talking about marketing ploys. I'm talking about looking at the way we live and how it will affect our future generations.

Today's eighteen to twenty-four-year-olds are the most future-phobic and anxious in recorded history. Yet ask them what they want, and they find an articulate voice. They will tell you they want to make a positive difference. They want to see an end to homelessness. They want to see a fairer distribution of wealth. They want to see the planet restored. They want to see our cities reflect the ideas of young people: more greenery, better functioning public transport, and city centres where people are inspired and where people of all ages gather, meet, and talk.

A few billionaires lead the world because they fund politics. If you fund politics with private funds, then you get governments acting on behalf of a tiny proportion of the population.

That is plainly absurd.

In recent years, we have seen the impact of that.

Politics has become a very dirty business. Narcissism has trumped intelligence, and national interest has come before global interest.

Ask yourself, 'Who is paying for me to see what I am seeing? And whose interests are they representing?'

CHAPTER 1

We've Got it Wrong

I was born to a Scottish-Irish father and a Lebanese mother who had grown up in Egypt. So, it was quite a mix to be born into as a cultural being. I spent three years in Pakistan between the ages of three and six-and-a-half. On the way back to Scotland, we almost got caught in Egypt. It was at the time of the Suez Crisis with the British government. I remember the troops on the shore of Port Said; we got out not long before the Suez Canal was closed.

I came back to Scotland, which I barely knew because I had travelled to Pakistan at age three. I found it cold and grey.

Settling into school was extraordinarily difficult for me because I had started kindergarten in Lahore, Pakistan. Evidently, I spoke pretty decent, rudimentary Urdu. I can only remember a few words of it now. It's so incredible how children absorb information in extraordinary ways because they are so adaptable.

I ended up attending a total of four different primary schools, and I hated it. I hated the whole school experience.

When I went to high school, it wasn't any better. I just could not settle myself. I was fidgety, distracted, disinterested, and bored. I was constantly thinking of the wider world, including the new music and ideas being circulated at the time. I was obsessed with the Beatles, the Rolling Stones, and being a rock star. I wanted to stand on stage, and at the age of fourteen, that's exactly what I did. I started a band. At school, none of that counted for anything because we were judged entirely on academic grounds. So, it was no surprise that, by the age of fifteen, I was asked to leave school on no uncertain terms.

If only I could have shown my former head teacher how I came alive on stage. How I felt this almost overpowering surge of adrenalin and how my confidence would soar.

My parents were going through a divorce, and it was horrible. They seemed to be living in different worlds. It didn't feel like home anymore, and it was hellish to be caught in the middle. Eventually, I escaped to London to get away from it all. I got a job in a shop selling furniture, and it was all going well until it wasn't. Apparently, none of the customers could understand a word I said because of my Scottish accent.

So, I was sacked three weeks into my first job there.

I ended up sleeping out for about a year, which was quite formative both in negative and positive ways. It was a challenging and threatening experience where I learned that I could survive and started to find out who I was as an individual. After that, I went through an extraordinary journey. I met a couple of Irishmen, and we headed off to their home city of Dublin. I was the first guitarist on the streets of Dublin, where I busked (played music and sang in public) and connected with the band Thin Lizzy. I became friends with Phil Lynott, the bass guitarist and lead singer, and Brian Downey, the drummer.

I had a succession of jobs before my twenty-sixth birthday, including bricklayer's labourer, steelworker, wine bottler, hod carrier, hospital orderly, biscuit packer, and community worker.

I also enjoyed a stint as a musician and actor.

I went to college in Scotland when I was twenty-two, and academically I was not lacking in anything. I did well in English literature. I found myself loving poetry, and I could write a really good essay. I was enthralled by politics and government. This additional education helped me to get a job as a community worker. It was then that I found that my period of homelessness was also a vital piece of my education.

We set up a housing association, which did up the old tenements and made them available as affordable flats. It was amazing to see how people, given the chance, could really excel.

CHAPTER 2

Greed

When it comes to greed, we can pin it down to three things these days: business, money, and politics. We've allowed business to kind of morph into unfettered greed, and we've allowed greed to grow. Business is a force for good, and business should be a force for good. The market can solve problems, and yet we've allowed it to get out of control. We now have a situation where the sixty-four richest people in the world, multi-billionaires, own more than the entire bottom half of the global population. They see themselves as successful. Yes. Okay. Many have had great business ideas, implemented them, and grown their companies exponentially. In the digital world, we are talking of a scale that is unprecedented. There comes a point when they are making money by simply having money. I don't think they're earning it. I think it's spurious to claim that people are earning it, and it is so much money that they can't even spend it within their lifetime. The worst part is that they keep charging the rest of us higher and higher prices. That's what I mean by greed.

We are living in really difficult times. The voices that will be heard come from people asking audacious questions. We need answers to those questions.

Everyone witnessed the profiteering during the height of the COVID-19 pandemic. Governments gave contracts to their friends, who then turned around and charged exorbitant amounts of money for stuff that was never even used because it was imperfect. This happened across the UK. That was greed beyond any sense of moral boundary. Scotland actually did better. It had a much better procurement system, and it paid less per unit than the rest of Britain.

It's time to rebalance our understanding of what money is about.

Money gives us good things and allows us to live in comfortable homes. It allows us to have green space around us, nice things, and the freedom to travel with money in reserve. Beyond that, money is merely a tool for narcissism. And worse yet, it becomes a tool to support governments.

Politicians are elected with money and are mainly made by money. That means that power and control are held by people who have exercised the greatest greed. That is where the problem lies in much of the world. So that is where we are at the moment.

We need to separate money from politics.

The best leaders are people who live in some of our most impoverished communities because leadership becomes a necessity to survive. People seem to think there is some kind of leadership gene. There isn't. We've allowed bad leadership in politics. Now we get to reroute politics to the communities where we live. That's where the power should be, because the people are sovereign. It's the very foundation of democracy.

We've gone beyond that.

The Scandinavian countries operate on a different political platform. They are the most successful countries in terms of closing the gap. They are the most advanced in terms of tackling climate change. They are the most progressive in terms of tax systems, and they are also consistently socially democratic. Their parties are aligned in parliament according to the proportion of votes they get. They have to beat things out, they have to argue, and they have to agree on a pathway. It's very consistent; you don't have this roller coaster before you and then another roller coaster. That type of system doesn't allow people to rest easily. It doesn't allow things like health and education to be stable fundamentals of a decent society.

CHAPTER 3

Damaged Our Planet

The world is not a settled place. What we do in the northern hemisphere greatly affects the southern hemisphere, first. The world is connected, and the earth is connected. There's a domino effect. Whatever we do as individuals affects others as well as the planet.

Greed has damaged our planet, and big oil companies have known that for a very long time. People on Earth have a limited time span; the earth will flourish when we are gone. However, we are tipping the scales to such an extent that even the earth may not survive.

Destroying the Brazilian rainforest is greedy and exacerbates climate change. It's also a political decision to do that. We now know this, even though there are people who argue against it. I say to them, "Ninety-nine percent of the scientists across the world all agree on the fact that we are doing damage to the planet.

So, why are some politicians willing to put future generations to the sword?

In my late teens and twenties, I saw things very clearly—without clutter, preconceptions, or political alliances. That's the type of clarity we have when we are young. That's why it makes perfect sense to include the younger generations in helping us solve those problems. In fact, it's critical to include our youth as part of a solution now, not waiting for the problem to grow to the point where they have to scramble into a boat.

One of the things that I find in my work with schools is that when I ask the students to draw a picture of the city they would like to live in, they draw cities that we should be living in now.

We shouldn't have political opposition to the things that need to be done, especially when we know they can be done. We know that Curitiba, in southern Brazil, is one of the most revered eco-cities in the world. Accessible public transport, plenty of green space, and recycling that's way ahead of anywhere else in the world. They also have 64 percent of the poorest part of the population now working in a very lucrative construction industry, so the average earnings are up as well.

Mayor Jaime Lerner's vision was a city designed for people; it wasn't about reducing carbon emissions. Now, what's interesting is that it also wasn't about reducing the number of cars. It was a city designed for people, and by the very nature of that vision, it meant reducing carbon emissions and making sure waste didn't go into landfills. He made some very imaginative things happen. Instead of building expensive and difficult-to-maintain levee systems, Curitiba purchased the floodplain and made parks. Rather than mowing with tractors, Mayor Lerner's innovative response was "municipal sheep," which keep the parks' vegetation under control and whose wool funds children's programmes. He created a programme that traded bags of groceries and transit passes for bags of trash. He also began a programme that paid fishermen by the pound for any garbage they retrieved. This way, they are able to make money even outside of the fishing season. In other words, if you want people to follow government policy, then make it worthwhile. Let them see what the vision is going to look like and how their children will benefit in the future.

The savings for Curitiba are in the millions.

Lerner instituted many innovative social and educational programmes as well. Bairro kids can be apprenticed to city employees if they want to avoid going to school.

The government takes glacial amounts of time to make things happen. Mayor Lerner asked his operations department how long it would take to pedestrianise a street (no cars allowed), and they said three to six months. He said, "I want it done in forty-eight hours." Did they get it done in forty-eight hours? Yes, they did. And of course, it was seen as an immediate success. All the neighbouring shopkeepers came to him and said, "People are spending more money. People are staying longer. People are relaxed. Kids aren't tethered to their parents. We want that as well." And it created a huge city-wide transformation.

When asked how he achieved this extraordinary turnaround, Mayor Jaime Lerner answered, "Take one zero off the budget, and you have creativity. Take two zeros off the budget, and you have genuine sustainability. But you have to beat off the complexity sellers."

A child will say, "I want a city that is designed for all of us." And an adult might say, "Where is the budget coming from? Can we do it? There's too much opposition." They tend to take a position that's going to be immediately adversarial.

Changemakers around the world draw people in because they don't complicate things with policies and facts. They just say, "We want a city designed for people and all those plants and creatures that inhabit the world".

I do believe in young people, and I'm at the age where so many of my contemporaries are dissing them and referring to them as "snowflakes".

This is a political weapon to attack young people and people who are more liberal-minded. This really is an attack tactic. We get to close the gap between the very wealthy and the poor because the current situation is absurd. Who does it serve to have more than half the global population living in poverty? It doesn't make sense for business; it doesn't make sense for the environment; it doesn't make sense for any part of humanity. It's actually a drain on society. It's insane and depressing.

When we mention poverty, some people argue that it's not abject poverty; real poverty is not knowing where the next meal is coming from. Well, actually, we have people who don't know where the next meal is coming from. So, we have a problem that must be addressed now. There must be some leverage from the money that has been amassed in tax havens. Britain specialises in tax havens. Money is moved out of London into bank accounts in the Cayman Islands, Bermuda, and places like that. This is actually a global issue, not just limited to Britain and the USA.

We get to stop that, and the world needs to agree on this now. The two countries that will oppose it most vociferously will be the US and the UK. The European Union wanted to address this, so what did the UK do when Europe started talking about closing off access to tax havens? They said, "We want to leave the EU," and that's what's happened. We still have time to address this. It's part of the process of repairing the world.

There's actually a great deal of enthusiasm to do that. The only stoppers are those who have a vested interest in retaining the status quo.

CHAPTER 4

Let the Young Flourish

I believe young people should be involved in local and national politics. It might add more voices to the cacophony of politicians, and yet we need to hear those voices. We need to give young people a sense that they are part of the solution, and we need to listen to them now. In Scotland, during the 2014 referendum, sixteen and seventeen-year-olds who were given the vote for the first time engaged in intelligent and serious debates. I was so impressed by the clarity of their contributions. They had done their research and were confidently engaged.

Reforming democracy sounds complicated. It's not. In Norway, when young people were leaving a small town because industry was being lost, the local government engaged the youth as part of the political solution. That's the thing to do. It's also about asking the right questions. For example, "What's going to encourage you to stay in this town?"

Every human being has enormous capacity. When you see it in children, you realise just how great that capacity is. In 2001, Kiran Bri Sethi founded the Riverside School in Ahmedabad, India. Kiran designed the primary school's curriculum and built it from the ground up. This all came about after dissatisfaction with her five-year-old son's education. Her early training as a designer is clear in her work as an educator—she looks beyond what exists and asks, "Could we do this a better way?"

Riverside School became a lab to prototype and define a design process that could consciously infect the mind with the "I can" bug. What Kiran uncovered was that if learning is embedded in real-world contexts, which means blurring the boundaries between school and life, this directly increases a student's wellbeing.

The children became more competent and less helpless.

When her fifth-grade class was learning about child rights, they were told to roll incense sticks for eight hours to experience child labour. In just two hours, after their backs began to ache, they were changed. Once that happened, they were out in the city, convincing employers that child labour had to be abolished and why.

The parents weren't convinced until they were shown how much the children's grades had improved later that year. Riverside School outperformed the top ten schools in India in math, English, and science.

Once this model was taken outside of the school, Ahmedabad became the first child-friendly city. Some of the children persuaded the local Metropolitan Council to close down the city one day every other month and hand it over to children. This idea has spread across India. Kiran has done a TED talk, and it's really interesting to hear how one activity with her grade 5 students created a movement for all of India.

Kiran is the founder of Design for Change (DFC), the world's largest movement of change for children by children. She is proving that children have an enormous capacity to educate their elders. They are even educating their elders, who cannot read or write.

We tend to keep young people compliant. "Listen to us; we know best," rather than hearing their ideas. I've been in primary schools, asked questions, and had children design posters. One of those campaigns was to reduce the consumption of alcohol in their neighbourhood. They came up with powerful wording for the campaign posters based on: 'When I see Mum and Dad drink, it means broken promises.'

Now, you don't think of that as an adult.

When we put that campaign into a play, the parents just sat open-mouthed. They had been caught. They didn't think that a child had enough sophistication to realise what was happening.

For example, a parent might say, "We'll do that next week, darling, and it will be bigger and better when we do". Then nothing happens, and they figure their child will forget about it. They don't, and they feel badly let down. Children are picking up things all the time and continue to remember how they feel when adults let them down.

So, when we start exploring the creativity and imagination of all parts of the community, we find richness. I have been able to do this. I have worked with people and communities. I have held big idea sessions and shown groups of people how extraordinary ideas have taken root around the world.

Creative People

Creative people with imagination see things that other people don't see. Henry Ford said, "If I'd asked people, I would have had to create faster horses". This opens the door for people to say, "Right. Nothing is too daft. Nothing is too stupid."

When you're a child and you share a creative idea, people say, "Listen, wait 'til you're old enough and wait 'til you're bringing in money before you start thinking about things like that."

I say, "Nonsense!"

If we allow imagination and creativity to flourish among young people, it will continue into adulthood. Most people reach adulthood, and their creativity has been stripped out of them. They are only educated from the neck up.

We routinely strip humanity of its greatest asset, which is the ability to create something that has value.

And yet, we can start putting things right today. We don't even need to wait for tomorrow.

CHAPTER 5

Chance to Put Things Right

Let's start having big creative sessions all over the world. That's what I enjoy doing. Perhaps we will find the next Einstein in an impoverished community somewhere in the world.

Young people aren't getting the chance to speak up; even with an education, no one gives them a chance. When we see a spark lit in them, we see young people accomplish astonishing things.

Anything human is possible, and when you think of the extraordinary things that humanity has achieved over the years, it's incredible. We get to break through the impasses that are besetting the world today. We get to start saying, "No more; we want to find positive solutions. We don't want to fight wars over it. We don't want great political battlegrounds."

It's good to argue about not having so many poor people in the world.

No one's going to argue with water shortages being a real problem, which in places like Africa would drive more refugees around the world than we have right now. People complain about refugees arriving on their shores. You get to add it all together. It's like a jigsaw puzzle. Work out a way to allow people to stay in their home countries. In order for this to happen, they need fresh water, safe homes and environments, a means to make a living, freedom, a good education, and a voice.

We get into this complexity of policies and procedures and think we need to have a huge budget. Ideas cost nothing, and they have no hierarchy. Right now, we are giving the freedom to have ideas to the people who run the money in the world.

I'm always ready to talk about the world, but we cannot sit and talk forever. It's about going out and doing things. That takes audacity, creativity, and leadership.

Leaders need to engage people in their vision. They should be brave, creative, and clear. I believe that soft power is the new hard edge and that we need to learn how to communicate all over again.

In order to make the world a better place, we need to address climate change, invest in education, and ensure access to health care. We can only do this by reducing the gap between the very wealthy and the very poor. This is not about taking money away from anyone, it's about redistribution of wealth and appropriate leadership.

Good leadership is about ensuring that the people you lead have dignity by making sure they know they are valued and that their ideas and contributions are significant.

Democracy is a system of government in which laws, policies, leadership, and major undertakings are directly or indirectly decided by the 'people'. We don't have democracy in its traditional understanding of demos, the Greek word for people and politics.

True democracy is of the people.

People are afraid to put their heads above the parapet. I've never been afraid to put my head above the parapet. And I do take people on. I've actually just recently offered politicians my help in getting them to communicate in a far more efficacious way. At the moment, it is all about policies, and people don't care about policies; they care about impact. Too many businesses have also been run on the basis of processes rather than outcomes.

We need big, audacious ideas that create a vision for a better world. Then we need to work backwards from that vision to where we are today. This will give us a map for moving forward. There is an urgency about this. We need to get leaders to make big decisions. Even if those big decisions are supported by employees, the problem comes with shareholders, who have a singular interest in getting their dividends. That seems to be the case.

We now know that investment in renewables creates far greater returns than investment in oil. So that's a positive. If we're going to invest, we must make sure those investments are ethical ones. This is something that we can change almost overnight.

Companies should have a different kind of balance sheet. The balance sheet shows what they are contributing to the world and how they are making a profit. We need the equivalent of a glass door for all companies, especially massive global companies.

This lack of accountability is threatening the very axis of the world. We've got to make sure that leadership now makes those demands. This is not a request; it is a demand. We need to see every company's open statement about their profits, investments, and the efforts they are making to improve the earth in terms of climate change as well as education. We need to be contributing to education at every level because learning is the way out of these situations.

I believe that people feel alienated from the world of politics. And when you've got alienation, you get changed behaviors; you get people giving up, which makes them easier to control.

When people don't have hope, everything begins to crumble.

The real effort on all our parts is to talk to leaders about legacy. What are they going to leave behind? What's their name going to suggest to future generations? This is a chance for millionaires and billionaires to ask themselves, 'What is my legacy going to be? How are people going to be talking about me in the future?'

I think about my own legacy, and I'm very far from a millionaire. In fact, I'm at the opposite end of the spectrum. I still have a sense of pride that when my name is mentioned in the future it's going to be a positive acclamation: 'This guy did something that was decent for the world; he spoke up for people; he wasn't afraid to speak out; he spoke to large audiences; he lifted spirits and gave people a sense that they have power—that they have ideas and that the world needs those ideas.'

Those ideas need to be reflected in what politicians do.

CHAPTER 6

Close the Gap

It happened one night in Piccadilly Circus. I was seventeen years old and wandering the streets in search of a place of warmth, just somewhere to lay my head down for the night. This led to an encounter that has never left me.

It was cold, and a charity pulled up in a van to offer me a warm bed for the night. So, I was taken to a big hostel. I was shown into a green-tiled room. I'll never forget that room. I was told to take my clothes off, which I did. When I looked up, there was a hose pointed at me and unleashed from top to bottom, back to front. I felt humiliated, spent a night at the hostel, and escaped back into the streets, so I wasn't taken to a holding house. I had no idea what that meant, and I didn't want further humiliation. At least on the streets, I had some dignity.

It wasn't the words spoken that night; it was the words not spoken.

You see, like many homeless people, my priority was not accommodation. It was to feel valued, to feel significant, to have a name, to have a history, and to have dreams, even if those dreams weren't forthcoming.

Step forward a few years. I'd been working at building sites all around London. Like many employees at the time, I'd had the full wrath of negative words bosses used: "you're not paid to think; that's above your pay grade; don't answer me back; if you make a mistake, you'll get a tonne of bricks falling on you."

One day I was assigned a new building site. I arrived early in the morning, eager to work. A Welsh foreman greeted me; he was sporting a tattered hat and had a nose that had obviously been broken several times. Reaching out his shovel-like hand, he grasped mine in a firm handshake.

Wrapping an arm around my shoulder, he said, "Welcome Michael." He took me to a small building and said, "Before you start, I want to show you something." Showing me the plans, he said, "This is the palace you're building". 'A palace?' Suddenly, I felt this incredible energy rising up. He had opened up a different kind of workplace because I saw a purpose. I saw myself contributing to this glistening new building that would rise into the London skyline.

That night, I went to meet my friends in the pub. They were all slumped at the bar, looking down at their pints. "What are you so chirpy about?", they said. "Guys, I'm building a palace!" It was that powerful. A few weeks after that, the same foreman pulled me aside at the end of the day and said, "Michael, will you do me a favour?" and I said, "Yes, of course". He handed me these keys and said, "I'm going to be late tomorrow; will you open the site for me?" There were all of these valuable materials lying about, and I said, "Me, open up the site?" He said, "Yes, I trust you".

As I left the site, tears rolled down my cheeks. No one had ever said they trusted me. That was the power of those words. I clutched the keys close to me in case I lost them. I barely slept that night. The next morning, I went into work early and opened the site. I felt that I had an elevated responsibility. It was an enormously important moment hearing the words, "I trust you". He also said, "Well done".

I was definitely changed as a result.

Language really does matter. When I look at how words denigrate and how we use them to take people down, to insult and wound them, sometimes fatally, I get to remember that we've got the same power with words to lift, elevate, motivate, and empower people.

Every day, we choose hundreds of words as we interact with others. How many lift and inspire people? How many have the reverse effect? In today's world, too much poison is poured on others: think social media comments; think arguments; think close relationships.

Do you lift or sink spirits?

The power we have with the words we choose when we are speaking or writing can be an empowerment tool for others. I've felt the ill winds of criticism, and I never want to experience that again. Ever. Words are that powerful.

CHAPTER 7

Start Nursing the Planet

A global imperative and three seeds of hope begin by considering our oceans, the fashion industry, and the importance of pure water. Over seventy percent of the Earth's surface is covered by saltwater oceans. Our wellbeing is totally dependent on those same oceans, and not just for beachside fun and seafood.

The world of fashion may glitter with temptation, but it leaves in its wake exploited, abused, and impoverished communities and a fast-depleting planet.

Can you imagine not being able to draw water from a tap? Most of us cannot conceive of water as a luxury, yet across the world, more than 1.2 billion people have no access to clean drinking water. And the situation is getting worse.

Seed #1 - Oceans Alive

The oceans help us breathe by producing half our oxygen; they absorb fifty times more carbon dioxide than the atmosphere and provide ingredients for medicines used to fight cancer, arthritis, Alzheimer's, and heart disease. How have we repaid this favour? By dumping eight million tonnes of plastic into the sea every year, contributing to acidity, global warming, and overfishing.

More than a million birds and one hundred thousand sea mammals and turtles die each year from eating plastic waste or getting tangled in it. We are waking up to the global imperative to keep our oceans free of pollutants, allowing them to help us live healthily—as they have since the birth of time. Humanity depends on it.

Seed #2 - Fashion and the Environment

We now face a new phenomenon called "greenwashing". This is the deceptive art of false labeling—giving the buyer the impression of an ethical supply chain with low environmental impact. The acceleration toward sustainable fashion is one of the most exciting and creative industries around, delivering on three main areas: restoring to the planet what we use in natural resources, revitalising the economy in those communities where cheap and disposable labour has been exploited for too long, and imaginatively reviving clothes once worn.

The reasons are clear. For far too long, we have worn the latest in-fashion clothes, then quickly discarded them as trends. It has one of the shortest life cycles of any product—from a few nights out on the town to landfills. Each purchase has already contributed to immense human damage and helped endanger our planet.

Sweatshops, low wages, and the exploitation of women and children have created a human crisis in some of the world's poorest communities. The industry's environmental impact is off the scale— it produces ten percent of all humanity's carbon emissions, is the second-largest consumer of the world's water supply, and pollutes the oceans with microplastics.

There is now a movement that will see communities in Lagos, Nigeria and Budapest, Hungary—move from being economically exploited to fashion producers earning a fair return on their labours, thus injecting growth into the local communities.

Seed #3 - Nothing on Tap

Water scarcity is one of the biggest challenges facing our world, with more and more regions without access to water for at least one month of the year. At last count, a fifth of the world's population had limited access to fresh water. There is enough fresh water in the world for its seven billion inhabitants, but it's distributed unevenly.

No water means no growth, and no growth means no food.

There are some imaginative solutions being found. Water drawn from the atmosphere, water purification and transportation projects, and the creation of wells in parts of the world where it is possible.

Global warming is a major cause of water shortages, making life unlivable for billions of people and other species. If we don't act to address this, many parts of the world will see their populations die or be forced to flee.

Places Where People Flourish

Words are words. Actions are actions. For example, you hear the phrase "sustainable communities" a lot these days—especially among professionals and politicians. But what does it mean for our lives?

Imagine a different way of living: You reside in a warm, comfortable home that doesn't take away from the earth and has no heating bills to pay. It's free. You have a job that pays you well or access to enough to keep you. When you leave your home, you see trees, greenery, and spaces to relax and breathe. You have shops and public transportation within easy reach. People walk and cycle freely.

Your children grow up happy, safe, healthy, and confident because opportunities to play are close and abundant. They get the best education and have choices about their future. As a result, they are invested and stay in their community. They, in turn, have children who can flourish. The air is clear, and nature can also flourish. That is a sustainable community in a nutshell.

Great words. Now for great actions.

CHAPTER 8

Give Leadership to Young People

The aftermath of COVID, the ever-dawning reality of climate change, rising income inequality, the war in Ukraine, and political leaders under legal investigation—is it any wonder that we have unprecedented global anxiety?

Despair not. Just read the room and respond positively, creatively, and speedily. Here are four ways workplaces can get creative and give leadership to young people:

The new 'F' Word is Fun

The Zoomers, or Generation Z, put fun as their number one value today. How can we create workplaces that offer slices of fun? What about installing a fireman's pole linking office floors, designing brighter décor, and creating several chill spaces? There are lots of opportunities to respond quickly and cheaply.

Productivity? Watch it rise while turnover and absenteeism fall. The evidence is there.

Stepping-Forward, Stepping-Up

After years of relentless self-improvement, self-transformation is now the order of the day. Mental health is spoken about openly. People, especially young people, put their hands up to express their feelings.

Workplace learning doesn't have to be directly job-related.

Help employees grow emotionally, spiritually, and socially—in turn, you will increase their overall capability, self-confidence, and emotional intelligence. Opportunities to provide life skills will also be appreciated.

Market 'Values' Before Product

Market segmentation used to be about simple demographic calculations. Now it is about reaching customers that align with what you stand for—how you view and respond to the growing disparities across the country, the climate crisis, and the welfare of your employees.

Around seventy-eight percent of consumers report a willingness to switch brands, and global consumers echo that high standard in their own lives and shopping behaviour as well. Eighty-four percent of consumers globally say they seek out responsible products whenever possible, though eighty-one percent cite the availability of these products as the largest barrier to purchasing more.

How can you represent your values and beliefs in new and imaginative ways? The creative force within.

For years, businesses have sourced inspiration from outside. Why not look within for differentiating ideas?

I have led creative events with employees across all sectors. These events are brilliant for sourcing all manner of big ideas from employees about products, services, and customer relationships.

Innovations spring up, and employees feel more valued.

CHAPTER 9

Human Beings

There is one category in which I can confidently divide people into two groups. Those that love what they do, and those that do what they do to get paid and just can't wait for the weekend. That means that in the workforce today, there are many thousands of people who simply go through the motions of working day-to-day.

What saddens me is that many haven't yet discovered their true talents and are not connected with themselves or others. You can see it in their eyes.

The 'eyes' have it.

We talk about the bright penetrative quality of a cat's eye or the sad, doleful eyes of a dog, yet we rarely speak of the power of the human eye. Through our eye contact, we establish trust and intimacy, convey empathy and understanding, and express interest or disinterest.

Our eyes smile, and they frown. Even the smallest changes in expression and movement speak loudly. No words are needed to make a powerful statement.

Have you ever been in a group meeting when the person talking fixes their gaze on you, totally to the exclusion of others in the room?

Awkwardness all around.

I have seen this so many times in my business and personal life. Eyes are a powerful tool and a vital conduit between us and the people around us.

As a speaker, my eyes play a huge part in how I communicate with an audience. First, I look at the people I am talking to. All of them. Sometimes individually focused. Sometimes scanning. Why would anyone listen if my eyes were averted to a PowerPoint, the floor, or the ceiling? When I look at you, I value and include you. That is the most basic of courtesies in most Western cultures. If I am passionate, my eyes light up—they speak with excitement and enthusiasm. In some cultures, no eye contact shows courtesy.

On a serious note, I might fix my gaze to convey gravity. On stage, it's called technique. In daily communication, our eyes speak just as powerfully. When we learn to use words, we are rarely taught how to use our eyes as part of our delivery.

If anyone doubted the importance of eye contact, the age of Zoom has surely taught us a valuable lesson. At first, our eyes were darting all over the screen. We looked swivel-eyed and slightly mad. It certainly took me a while to look at the camera, not the person. It was counterintuitive.

Our instinct is to want to see the whites of people's eyes. Eyes truly are a window into another person's world.

Not a Dry Eye in the House—As for My Pants?

I learned how to engage an audience at the age of eight, and it's an experience I never want to repeat. I was to sing 'Tit Willow' from the Mikado at my primary school concert. Shaking with fear, I was pushed onto the stage by a teacher. Then, as I attempted my first notes, the floodgates opened and I peed myself—my grey shorts turned a shade darker, and a small pool gathered on the stage.

When someone ran on with a mop and bucket, my humiliation was complete. In truth, it was a brilliant engagement technique. All eyes were on me.

But please! Never again.

As a speaker for more years than I care to count, I have found a less embarrassing way to quickly engage an audience. When I step on stage, I don't rush to speak; I don't greet the audience, offer an explanation, or introduce myself. I pause and then tell a story.

Silence is engaging.

Words, Words, Words

Words can poison, denigrate, sink, and sometimes fatally wound. They are the most powerful human tools. We can also use them to lift, empower, encourage, motivate, and inspire.

Each of us remembers the words spoken to us. For some of us, they compounded a sense of worthlessness and drove us further into a downward spiral. For others, they were the spark that ignited belief, confidence, and progress. Here starts my mission: to rediscover our positive power through the words we use.

Have you heard of the 'Gish Gallop?

It's a hideous persuasion technique that's been used by some politicians in recent times. You've seen it in play. Gish Gallop's name comes from American creationist Duane Gish, who used this approach to argue against scientifically proven evolution.

Do you recognise the following tactic?

The perpetrator uses a rapid series of spurious arguments, half-truths, misrepresentations, and outright lies—all in a short space of time. The idea is to render their opponents unable to refute so many claims and make them look weak.

When I train people in persuasive speaking, I give examples of this as the worst kind of manipulation that has won elections. So, it's dangerous.

We get to return to honest and positive persuasion: the skill of painting a vision, using words and concepts that people understand, and being clever as well as creative in delivery.

I regard this as the must-have skill of this century.

Indecision

Indecisiveness costs the economy and saps morale. When we prevaricate, time and opportunity pass.

We know that if we place a storage box in the corner of a room and don't move it in three days, it stays there for over six months. When we hold off on those minor repairs around the house, we begin to tolerate broken lights, malfunctioning door knobs, and unfinished painting projects until it's time to sell the house. We finally get the home we want on our way out.

When we are decisive, it prevents the wretched anxiety of prevarication.

When a leader sits on a decision, people see it, smell it, and feel it—

indecision is now in full play. It spreads across an organization and faith is lost.

If you are not trusted to make decisions, you are not a leader people will follow.

Perhaps that's why seventy percent of employees now feel disconnected from their employer.

CHAPTER 10

Endless Capacity

As humans, we have an endless capacity to do good and to do what is right. In order to create something better, we need a clear global purpose. Right now, we are very fragmented between self-interest and what our responsibilities are to the people around us.

Deep down, we are amazingly resourceful.

Some of the best initiatives around the world have been done without a budget and have saved a lot of money. In South Africa, I visited an art class in a township school, where I saw some exquisitely crafted models made from scrap materials gathered in the neighbourhood. For example, a tiny wheelbarrow with wheels that worked, airplanes made from cardboard, and human figures made from wire. In Paraguay, a music teacher with no budget for instruments made them from scrap material. The school now has a performing orchestra.

As adults, we often think we need money to do things, children don't. They merely use their imaginations. When we do, we increase sustainability for the planet.

Embrace Cultural Diversity

I am so lucky to have inherited a rich blend of Celtic and Arabic influences. I used to smile inside when ridiculed by youngsters at school, and then slightly less frequently in early adulthood. I was a rarity in my younger years. Now I am one of millions who draw their inspiration and influence from a rich and colourful palette. I love being a mix of Scottish-Irish and Lebanese heritage. It is an intoxicating blend.

Celtic wit and stubbornness meet Lebanese hospitality.

I think it makes me a force to be reckoned with: refusing to bow to power, speaking with passion, ready to break the tension with biting humour, determined and resilient to the end, and able to wind down with a hookah.

I can switch from a brogue to a lilt to a Lebanese inflection in the same sentence. It keeps people on their toes.

We all love a good laugh, and the Scots and Irish have it in abundance. Then add in the Lebanese and their infectious laughter. I get to enjoy the best of both worlds. I'll raise a glass of whisky or Guinness and arak to that!

As for racism? Get a hold of yourself.

Get with the joys of cultural blending.

Let Laughter Ring Out at Work

Laughter is a brilliant business improvement tool. Leaders with humour are twenty-seven percent more motivating.

Their employees are...

-less stressed

-more productive

-more creative

-more approachable

Modern leadership promotes humour because it makes things better in every way. As a leader, it worked for me. As a speaker and consultant, I have seen huge impacts.

Top rule: Never belittle anyone.

Many years ago, I had a large housing association in England as a client and held a Ways to Improve Workshop. The receptionist said, "I get all the flack and anger, and I hate that." My solution was to play TV's 50 Funniest Moments on a big screen in the reception area. The results? Complaints were dramatically reduced. Frustration over waiting times was also dramatically reduced.

The final result? Happier receptionist.

Remember this: "You don't stop laughing when you grow old; you grow old when you stop laughing." ~George Bernard Shaw

Let Freedom Ring

Freedom is hard-fought and never to be lost. What change has had the biggest impact on your life? I asked this question to a hall full of students at Edinburgh Napier University.

As you might expect, the iPhone, Google, and a host of other technological advancements were listed. Then a quiet voice emerged from the back of the room. "Freedom of speech." This student was from Eastern Europe.

It was a sharp reminder that authoritarian governments silence their critics. What she had endured under an authoritarian government became the focus of discussion. For those of us brought up with freedom, it was an awakening. It also served as a reminder to democratic politicians that they are elected to serve, not rule.

Argument, dissent, and opposition are healthy.

Great leaders listen, digest, and argue their points with reason and compassion. If they have to rethink, amend, abandon, or change, they do so with grace and humility. They do not lie, bully, demonise, create false enemies, or try to silence their critics. They serve all the people, not just those who back them and support them. They remember that the word democracy is made up of two Greek words that together mean "people power".

CHAPTER 11

Creative & Imaginative

When chaos reigns, it is a sign of better things to come. This has certainly been the pattern of my life. Periods of sometimes desperate lows have been followed by highs. The lower the point reached, the higher the upward swing.

When I began to recognise this cycle, things changed.

First, I knew that however bad things got, better was just around the corner. That's an important lifeline. Then I asked myself if I could use this cycle to my advantage and prepare for the upswing.

When I hit rock bottom in 2012, I had lost my business. I had skyrocketing debts as a result of the loss of my business, house, and much more. I was relaxed about it and certain that I would bounce back. At sixty-two, many doubted I had the resolve, energy, or wherewithal. I got cracking on building my reputation as a speaker. I was helped by Axa Business Insurance featuring me in an advertisement and a number of TV and radio interviews.

"Are you that older guy I saw on BBC Breakfast?" I was asked on my journey back from Manchester's Media City. I figured if I could pull this one off, I would have an even better story to tell. Then came

COVID. Many gigs were cancelled, and a newly filmed ad and billboard campaign were shelved.

No one in the filmed audience wore a mask. Why would they? It has been a monstrous rollercoaster. Looking back, my whole life has been a metaphor for all of life.

The world is at a very low point today. As I predicted five years ago, this is the chaos needed for the clouds to clear and old orthodoxies to be consigned to history.

We are in a period of renewal.

Everything will look and feel different in five years. Let's focus on a vision of what that can be and start preparing for it.

I survived because I have always seen challenges as creative opportunities. The time is now ripe for the fearless, creative, and bold outliers of change. The changemakers and the thought leaders.

In Adversity There is Opportunity for New Leaders

It is no coincidence that most great leaders have experienced failure. Now is the time for them to step up. Adversity has a way of eliciting talents that would otherwise have remained latent.

I learned more from life's brutalities than from anything I have been formally taught.

Leadership is about harnessing the lessons of an imperfect life. One marked by failures and periods of despair. It builds resilience and develops humility, empathy, and resilience. It teaches you to never look down on people or claim superiority over others. You learn that what comes before all else is clarity of vision and values for living your life. You need a certain degree of magnetism. Those who have suffered have that.

The best leaders I have known came not from a classroom but from the cold, grey landscape of hardship. They learned that selflessness is a positive human attribute, and they worked hard to lift their brothers, sisters, and neighbours.

They saw the youngest in their midst as jewels to be shined and polished.

Great leaders value you with their eyes, actions, and words. They help you grow in their care. They represent all people under their influence, not just those who fuel their egos, and they judge their success and failure by the success and failure of others. They see the big picture and share it. They give hope without false promises, encourage others to fulfil their dreams, and work at building people up with the confidence to do so. They look up to others, not down on them. Their abilities do not come from schooling but from a life fully lived. That ability comes from being looked down on, given irrational instructions, and given low-impact tasks. From bosses being unclear about why they were doing a certain task or job, not sharing a clear vision, and using their position to belittle others.

Leadership is about inspiring others to overshoot their ambitions and become leaders in their own right.

I can think of no time in my life when great leadership has been in such short supply.

Recruiters must challenge the convention of hiring leaders whose education takes precedence over skills gained in adversity. Those who inspire passion understand humanity because they have experienced it from different perspectives.

Don't Typecast Us and Don't Downcast Us

On stage, I played a number of roles. A happy-go-lucky lothario, a

Jacobite (who dressed as a woman to escape the enemy), and a comedic hero.

In my short on-screen acting career, I appeared in a movie in which I played a brutal gangster with a gravelly voice and murderous intent. Then, I was in a TV detective series where I was characterised as a malevolent drinker.

Every casting offer thereafter picked up on my apparently gangster-like demeanour. I don't have one. I am mild-mannered and absolutely abhor violence. Don't get me wrong; I loved playing a gritty thug, but this sudden need to typecast me was irritating.

Once labelled, it's hard to escape—even with a concealed gun at the ready.

As a speaker, I am expected to be 'one-dimensional'. The world of business demands a niche. What is your keynote about? Who is the audience, and what are the challenges they face?

I understand why niche marketing is important. I owned a creative agency for twenty years, but I refuse to be one-dimensional. I am listed as a motivational speaker because whatever I speak about, I make it insightful, inspiring, and motivating.

My range is broad. I have lived many lives. So how can you expect me to fit into a tiny box? Why does this happen? We are conditioned to believe that multidimensional people are masters of nothing.

Nonsense.

CHAPTER 12

Anything is Possible

When a lionhearted girl was recognised by her peers but not her teacher, I was working with a class of sixteen-year-olds in an Edinburgh school. As a business owner who believes in investing in the local community, I was determined to use company resources to help nurture a new generation of confident and creative young people.

My aim on this occasion was to stretch the scope of possibilities ahead and put them in the driving seat of their destinies. As an exercise, I got them to complete the animal personality quiz. Also referred to as the Smalley-Trent model. The Four Animal Personality Assessment is a personality inventory created by Gary Smalley and Dr. John Trent that uses DiSC profiles to categorise people into four animal groups: lions, otters, beavers, and golden retrievers. The Lion is a leader, the Beaver a hard-working and diligent doer, etc.

It was a lighthearted exercise, and we had a great deal of fun.

The young people loved it and took pride in what the exercise might be saying about them. One of the girls scored very high on leadership. It was almost off the scale. She was a lion. "Oh," said the teacher in a lightly mocking way, "I wouldn't have described you as a leader."

The girl's classmates instantly responded by saying, "You should see her in drama class. She's a real leader. She helps us all." I loved that their instinct was to step in and talk her up. And that they recognised her leadership qualities. This was a mixed class of both boys and girls.

What really struck me was that as the conversation developed, it became clear that they saw her leadership as helpful, supportive, and guiding—not bossy.

There you have it.

Do we look for and recognise leadership in schools, and do we harness it? When we are crying out for great leaders, it helps little when teachers fail to recognise those qualities. When I was in school, it was the compliant students who were rewarded with leadership positions. We were never tested for leadership potential or taught how to lead.

What makes an extraordinary leader?

They use soft power and influence others with ease. It is a rare skill. When you learn how, you take your leadership to a whole new level. I am talking about 'extraordinary' new heights. It's great to have a clear vision, but the real trick is how to engage and excite people.

The best leaders wield soft power. They are erudite and creative in their communication. They maintain high morale and momentum.

Soft Power - The New Hard Edge

This story is about the old woman who inadvertently sold my house.

It was a glorious summer's day on the south side of Glasgow, and I was taking full advantage of the sunshine. There I sat in my front garden with a glass of white wine in hand, thinking of better days ahead.

Suddenly, there was a creak at my gate. I looked up, and there, slowly shuffling towards me, was an old woman. "Hello", I said. "Can I help you?" "Oh, son", she said, "I just wanted to tell you that this house is full of happiness and renewal".

"That's a lovely thing to say" I said.

"Och", she replied, "I was walking past and I had this sense of something special and wonderful coming from your home". By this time, I had established with her that I was the owner.

"Do you want a cup of tea or a glass of wine?" "No son. I just wanted to tell you that. I must go and see my grandchildren. They are expecting me."

So, she vanished.

It had indeed been a happy place for me. A year later, I chose to return to Edinburgh and start a new venture. The house was up for sale. The first, second, and third viewers were regaled with this tale.

All were enchanted, and a bidding war started. I did well on that sale. What great proof that a story is more powerful than facts and figures!

Soft power is using stories rather than stats, facts, figures, and lectures. It is the art of 21st-century leadership.

The World is On Edge

Only bold new ideas and the audacity to deliver against the grain will overcome the challenges we face. I believe creativity is the single most important human attribute.

Creativity gives us the ability to...

see what others can't.

conjure up alternative visions.

cut through intractable challenges.

Politics and Creativity Rarely Cross Paths

A scan of international cities radically transformed for the benefit of citizens reveals they were led by creatives who had gone into politics. They had ideas to excite and capture the imagination. They spoke the language of the people, but with big ideas. They rejected the naysayers and made budget availability the least important thing.

If anyone had told me when I was a teen in the 1960s that we would eventually be using artificial intelligence to enhance lives—using vertical farming in urban environments, seeing greenery in the desert, making advancements on dementia and neurological conditions, and so much more—I *would* have believed it.

I had an early escape from an education system that routinely dismisses our imagination as a useless pest. I saw a different world emerging in which people are central and tolerance abounds.

You see, children are endlessly curious and creative. They see no barriers as insurmountable and will find ways and means to overcome them. Because that is not nurtured throughout life, the ability to conjure up alternative realities is not common currency.

Rather, we choose to occupy intransigent positions and draw battle lines against those who disagree with us.

I believe that the next ten years can be a time of great creativity and innovation.

True Wealth

True wealth comes from the riches of our minds, not our pockets. Money merely facilitates a plethora of inspiration and life-enhancing ideas that are spreading across the globe. Research them, celebrate them, and tell others.

Why? Because the mainstream media won't.

What of our youth?

Too many are ridiculed when they raise ideas. Do not give naysayers oxygen to pollute their minds.

Generations of Scots have passed onto their children the 'don't get above yourself' belief. In Sweden, kids are taught not to be too much or too little, just enough. And in Australia, the young are told not to call attention to themselves—those who do are called Tall Poppies.

Timidity must be replaced by audacity.

Imagination and experience need to be mined. Young and old in the same room? Why not? That is where riches are to be found.

The answer is not to reach into the playbook of restructuring. It is to engage people (normally uninvited) and find solutions—however outlandish they seem.

Henry Ford, Walt Disney, and Alexander Graham Bell—each was mocked at first.

Audacity is at the heart of human progress. It is the courage to take risks, pursue dreams, and break boundaries. The courage to challenge the status quo and push beyond what we believe is possible is what makes progress happen.

Throughout history, countless individuals have faced adversity in order to bring about progress. From civil rights activists and suffragettes to entrepreneurs and scientists, many have put their ideas and dreams into action, despite the potential risks.

This is audacity at its finest.

Audacity is a necessary trait for progress. It is the willingness to take a stand and have faith in the power of change. This is what pushes boundaries and encourages creative thinking that can lead to new solutions.

Audacity is also about resilience—the courage to keep going despite setbacks and failures. It is the determination to keep trying, even when the odds seem insurmountable. It takes strength to get back up and keep going.

Audacity is at the heart of progress. It is a necessary trait for those who dream of a better future. It is through this courage and resilience that ideas become reality and human progress is made possible.

Don't dwell on what we do today or prevaricate on decisions.

To put our foot on the accelerator of progress, we need young people involved in shaping it today, not tomorrow. Don't shut down their ideas, as every previous older generation has done. Acceptance of inevitability is what we do as adults; fate induces paralysis. Don't expect a generation that understands the future better than we do to simply inherit what we have chosen to leave behind.

Elevate youth. Support them in understanding who they are as individuals. Recognise their wisdom. Open your heart to them and let them know you care.

It All Starts with Make Believe

Almost every positive development in our lifetime, started not with a spreadsheet or a plan. But with a flight of fancy. The flight of the creative mind. Time spent in the land of make believe.

The logical mind takes a different route.

It starts with budget availability, timescales, and appointment of a project team.

It sets outcomes.

It rejects most ideas because they are impractical and don't fit with priorities.

When Edi Rama, a painter, became Mayor of Tirana his big ideas would have had many political leaders shaking their heads.

"No, this is daft."

He saw a picture in his mind and brought it to life.

Picking a palette of colours, ordering thousands of trees, and instructing the cleanup of all civic spaces, he set about implementing his vision.

Painting the city's buildings—including all homes.

Planting fifteen thousand trees.

Revitalising all civic spaces.

Result: Delighted citizens, a feel-good factor across the city—and wait for it

Crime came down.

Who would have thought?

Challenges excite creatives.

They exercise logical thinkers.

CHAPTER 13

Everyone Has a Story

"Michael, I'm sorry to tell you that we no longer have a place for you at this school." My headmaster shuffled uncomfortably and paused briefly, brushing a few crumbs from his gown as he glanced sternly over his spectacles. "Perhaps the world of industry might offer you a future," he added without much conviction. I tried to mirror his frown, but this was a moment of long-anticipated joy for me, and impulse took over as my face broke into a broad grin. "Thank you, sir; it's been a pleasure," I said, not trying to disguise the cynicism in my voice.

Contemptuously, I left the door to his study wide open, breaching school rules, and ran as fast as I could down the corridor towards the exit, barging past an astonished Miss Morris, the ladies' advisor. Just a few weeks before, I'd trodden on her toes at the school dance, and she'd yelped dramatically before limping from the floor. My final gesture of defiance was payback for all the lectures she'd delivered over the years about my bad behaviour, my insolence, and the length of my hair.

As I ran through the school gates for the last time and into the warm embrace of the sun, a stiff breeze raced past me like it was escaping from something. It felt like freedom, and I ran after it as fast as I could. After years of what felt like captivity, my chains were finally broken, and I dreamed that I had the world at my feet.

I was beholden to no one, no longer forced to endure turgid lessons in algebra, battle dates by rote, and verb declensions reinforced by the thick end of a belt. The school's dreary cast of teachers had long since given up on me as a lost cause, just as I'd long since dismissed them as a bunch of uninspiring and vindictive system drones.

My school was in Scotland, whose reputation spanned the world as a cradle of enlightenment and the intellectual engine of the Industrial Revolution, and whose education system was lauded internationally as second-to-none.

Scotland has been home to people who shaped the ideas of the modern world. It was the land of great philosophers and political economists like David Hume, Thomas Carlyle, and Adam Smith—the father of capitalism. It produced giants of science, engineering, invention, and medicine and celebrated writers and poets like Robert Burns, Robert Louis Stevenson, Walter Scott, and James Boswell. It spawned innovators like William Galt and Charles Rennie Mackintosh and empire builders like Andrew Carnegie and William Reith, who founded and sustained great institutions using only the force of their intellect and sense of creativity.

All of those people had enjoyed the benefits of a Scottish education, which was the most solid grounding anyone could hope for—yet to this distracted young mind, information without inspiration just didn't register.

As the head teacher was pulling the shutters down on my school career in the summer of 1965, a younger pupil was being accelerated through the same school as part of an innovative, fast-track programme in academic 'hothousing'. Gordon Brown, the future Labour Prime Minister, would later cite the experience of attending my school as a personal case study in social mobility, demonstrating the value of his party's educational policies. His rise from humble beginnings, as the son of a church minister who enjoyed a stellar political career, was an edifying endorsement of a successful and meritocratic state education system. For him, Kirkcaldy High was the springboard from which he would go on to hold the two most senior offices of state, winning global renown and recognition.

My experience of the school was less edifying, and my unceremonious departure was the final act in a long-drawn-out tragedy. Regarded universally among the teaching staff as feckless, I'd been dismissed from a young age as beyond salvation. It wasn't just that they lacked the means to save me from the scrap heap; in those days, there was no such thing as learning support; they also lacked the will. It was a one-size-fits-all system, and if you didn't fit, then you were cast aside like a misshapen reject on a production line.

And once outside the system, there you would stay.

It's difficult to explain properly to anyone who didn't experience it what the education system of the 1950s and 1960s was like. It was a time of rigid standardisation when those who failed to keep pace simply ceased to exist. This was before the advent of the comprehensive model of schooling, which, for all its faults, was founded on a laudable desire to make every pupil count, no matter their background or ability.

The system I grew up in was binary and unwavering, promoting and rewarding the few it thought were bright enough to go on to higher education, while the rest of us were herded through a channel of lesser options, mostly in trades and clerical apprenticeships.

My experience was at odds with the cultural homogeneity of the time; this would have been enough of a problem in a major city, but in a small town, I might as well have flown in straight from Mars. And yet I could speak rudimentary Urdu. I knew how to peel a mango and ride a donkey. I'd sailed half-way across the world. I'd seen British soldiers with fixed bayonets stationed on the banks of the Suez Canal. I'd even been entertained by snake charmers. But those experiences counted for nothing, and they even drew rebukes from my teachers, who regarded my background as strange.

As I paused for one last glance at the grim crop of buildings that had held me hostage for the past three years, I didn't feel the faintest regret. I had no idea what I'd do, but with the innocence of youth, that was all part of the excitement. The future was mine to make or break. I'd dreamt of this moment for so long that I wanted nothing to spoil it. As I ran faster and faster, the asthma that had dogged me since birth kicked in, and I was forced to slow and then come to a stop. I found my inhaler, took two puffs, and without warning, I started to cry. The tears were genuine and heartfelt for a lost childhood—for the hundreds of sleepless, breathless nights I had endured; for the bedwetting and the constant anxiety; for the name-calling, sneering, ostracism, and violence of playground bullies; and for all the humiliations and punishments I'd endured at the hands of the teachers.

My family hadn't escaped from a less developed society with the aim of bettering themselves. I hadn't been raised in a poverty-stricken slum, and I didn't 'want for food' or proper clothing. My parents were educated; my father was a teacher and my mother was a stay-at-home mum. While they weren't affectionate or demonstrably loving, they did provide a comfortable life.

CHAPTER 14

Four Primary Schools

Standing with my hands and feet frozen, I surveyed the scene. Boys running, skipping, and kicking in temperatures below freezing—this was surely a super race, able to defy any climatic condition nature could throw at them. My feet and hands were frozen in submission.

Shivering would have been a luxury.

I wanted to feel the beating rays of the sun. I wanted sweaty palms. I wanted to shelter in the cool shade. I would have done anything at that moment to return to the tropics. I closed my eyes and imagined the sweating, pulsating streets of Pakistan. This was my first day at primary school in Scotland, where we were inhumanly shoved out into an arctic playground. It was hell on earth. It wasn't until Scotland had experienced its full weather cycle that I realised that these boys were mere mortals. As they sweated and sheltered from the impact of twenty-four degrees centigrade, I saw their vulnerability just as I had learned to disguise my shiver.

Months earlier, Pakistan's Lahore had been my home—the memories were etched deep. The searing heat, the street beggars, the spice markets, the sugar cane stalls, and the oxen carts vying with the internal combustion engine; the heavy cloudbursts, the cascading rain, the flooded streets, and that scent of rich humidity that hangs in the air as the sun reasserts its power The backdrop to life in Asia was dramatic. I remembered the vultures and kites as they shaded the sun and swooped on their helpless prey. I remembered the unrelenting and scorching sun, the cacophonous chorus of birds and crickets, and the sounds of donkeys laden with tins and cans. I remembered limbless, blind, and desperate beggars who clutched you in hope of a rupee.

I recalled the peacock colours of the women's saris: azure, rich sea blue, and vermillion—streets awash with bright colours and the scents of a million spices waiting in baskets to assault one's taste buds. Human enterprise was evident on every square inch of every street.

I remembered asking myself, 'Why does poverty smile?'

It took some time getting used to the bats crashing against the window shutters at night and the lizards that kept a constant insect watch as they sped up and down inside the walls and across the ceiling of our new home. It was life in full, vivid technicolour.

I was first sent to convent school, then shortly after to another primary along the road. I didn't fare well in the classroom. When we were meant to be reading from the blackboard, I couldn't see anything. Yet others were able to pick out words and images. When I was asked to read from it, I sat rooted to the spot. I couldn't say a word, and I was always in trouble for it. It took a while before an insightful teacher realised that perhaps poor eyesight was a contributing factor. Of course, one visit to the optician told the story. I was shortsighted, and all that pain and sense of inadequacy were totally unnecessary.

From then on, I was fitted with the aesthetically criminal, pink, national health spectacles with the coiled wire that wrapped around the ears. I could now see that damage had been done to my schooling—and my ego. I knew already that I hated school and could only look forward to the day when I would never have to enter one again. At only nine, I still had a few years to endure.

Then, just as I was getting accustomed to life in Edinburgh, Dad was offered a teaching post in Kirkcaldy, Fife. Another move, and this time our lives would never be the same.

1960 Kirkcaldy, with its population of fifty-seven thousand, is as far flung from Lahore as you can imagine. The streets were clean, and industrialization was dominated by the manufacture of linoleum—the smell of linseed oil used in its production permeated the atmosphere. My parents had purchased a grey brick house with, much to my delight, a garden at the back, complete with an apple and plum tree. A must for climbing, I thought mischievously.

Mum took charge of the décor, using a small inheritance she had received to carpet and furnish it to her taste. A year later, she was pregnant with my youngest brother, Tony. Eileen, Brian, and I were delighted. It didn't take Brian and I long to make our mark on the locality. Our neighbours, the Sharps, had three sons, and we quickly struck up a friendship with them. Sandy was Brian's age; Alan was the same age as me; and Russell was a year older. Our upbringing couldn't have been more different. They lived a typically Scottish Presbyterian existence. Their lives were centred in Kirkcaldy, and their father was our family doctor.

There, we could wander farther than in the city and quickly find nooks and crannies to fire our imagination. Our own garden gave us hours of pleasure, while just down the road, garage lockups offered us what seemed like a full-scale football pitch. Cowboys and Indians would clamber over the wall that divided our house from the Sharps. British soldiers would hide in the undergrowth, and on rainy days, we would assemble in our house and make up our own good, clean, prepubescent fun.

Brian was always ready for a bit of rough and tumble, while I was becoming more precious. The asthma attacks were increasing in frequency and intensity, and something wasn't right. I seemed to stand apart from the other boys, and while they ran endlessly, I had to pause and regain my breath. It was tricky.

St. Marie's is a small Roman Catholic primary school along the road. It was hardly surprising that I didn't fit in from the minute I arrived. My writing skills had been honed at school in Edinburgh, where written script was the convention. Now I was asked to convert to an italic style. That probably accounts for the eclectic and illegible form that characterises my written work now.

Thank heavens for the computer.

But that wasn't all I had to contend with. My teacher was a towering man at 6'5" who took an instant dislike to me. Maybe it was because my father was a teacher at the big school. He certainly made many dismissive references to him. Or maybe he just didn't fancy me.

He would seat boys on his knee and encourage them to snuggle up to him. At times, he would take boys home with him. Perhaps I should be grateful for his lack of affection for me, but I felt discarded at the time. I would ask myself why he didn't include me in any of his gatherings. I would watch enviously as other boys in the class would be given lavish praise and affection.

He seemed to despise me and, on occasion, would belt me or rattle my head against the blackboard. It was usually for sniffing during morning prayers or for fluffing my lines when we were asked to recite the catechism, the Catholic doctrine. That is probably when I finally decided that Catholicism would not feature in my adulthood. I hated school with such a passion that it is almost unbearable to think about it even now.

My teachers' admonishments were invariably accompanied by some ritualistic form of physical punishment, such as a slap on the head. Many teachers in those days considered physical punishment a method of first resort in the enforcement of discipline. The perpetration of violence against anyone in their charge was a right as far as they were concerned; some, I'm sure, regarded it almost as a perk of the job. The same treatment against an animal would have been frowned upon if not reported to the police, and yet, because it was carried out in a school in the name of educational discipline, no one thought there was anything wrong with it. If you were belted or slapped at school, which I was frequently, you certainly didn't tell your parents, as instinctively they would conclude that you had brought the punishment upon yourself and repeated it at home.

The weapon of choice for teachers was the "tawse"—a long, thick leather thong or whip, fashioned from coarse cattle hide, which had three prongs at one end for when greater pain was required to be inflicted. The preferred and most notorious manufacturer of the tawse was based in Lochgelly, a Fife town just a few miles from Kirkcaldy.

Today, being associated with such an instrument of torture would be brand suicide and an embarrassment for the town, but in those days it was a source of local pride.

Miscreant pupils were instructed to hold both hands outstretched with palms uppermost, one over the other, to provide support and prevent them from being able to move their hands as the strap came down. It also ensured that the full force of each stroke was taken by the hand being strapped.

The number of strokes delivered depended on the severity of the crime, and there were legends of past pupils having received twenty, thirty, or even forty lashes for the most trivial of offences, though in hindsight there was an air of urban myth about such stories. The most I ever received was six for sniffling during prayers on a morning when the school was being honoured by a visit from the local parish priest. I'd never experienced pain like that. Just a few strokes left a stinging sensation that made me feel like my hands were on fire.

My experience at St. Marie's was brutal and loveless.

I was not a natural rebel, but I seemed to attract the disapproval of those in authority without trying. I can't pretend I was the most industrious of students, but neither was I lazy, and I was far from being the class dunce. Just being myself, it seemed, was enough to provoke the annoyance of my elders and betters. On one occasion, I remember a teacher overhearing me telling a classmate about Pakistan, which resulted in a dressing down.

"Who the hell do you think you are, Stevenson?" he demanded. "You're in Scotland now. If you love Pakistan so much, why don't you go back there?"

To most of my classmates I was a curiosity and I remember being asked if my mother wore shoes. I resented my parents for uprooting me from Pakistan and moving us to this dark, grey, and challenging environment where the rain was cold and persistent and the food so unappetizing.

I saw the boys around me as part of some superhuman race because most of them were bigger than me and they didn't seem to be affected by the freezing temperatures. They didn't complain about their surroundings or about the bad treatment habitually meted out by the teachers, and they ate the appalling food with gusto and even demanded more.

My earliest friends at school were Italians or Poles, whose parents were post-war settlers. We clearly shared the sensibilities of an outsider. But friendships aside, I was miserable at school.

Already struggling to keep up, I soon found myself falling further behind in class. My parents were alerted to my lack of progress, which heaped greater pressure on me and made me feel scared and fearful, particularly because I had no clue as to why I appeared to find so difficult what my contemporaries appeared to take in their stride. The school clearly had no resources or strategies for dealing with me, and it offered my parents no solutions for how I might improve.

I could not understand what was happening and looked to myself for a reason. There must have been something wrong with me. I didn't discuss it with my parents at the time, and I used to suffer in silence. I was becoming more timid-and-withdrawn by the day, and my health suffered as a consequence. I became alone in my thoughts and fears. I would spend as much time as I could away from school and at home.

My mother would have friends over for regular coffee mornings, and I would find comfort in their company during my absences. The scent of their perfume and their confidence gave me strength. By age eleven, I began to experience the early awakenings of my own sexuality. The stocking legs and stiletto heels of my mother's friends were stirring something within me. I was too young to understand these physical reactions, but I knew that my relationship with my teacher was crippling me emotionally. I couldn't express myself for fear of being publicly ridiculed or beaten. It was a living nightmare.

I don't remember how it happened, but somehow the teacher was found out for his unhealthy interest in his male pupils and was instantly dismissed from his post. It turned out that he had been caught at his previous job for exactly the same offences. My father was incandescent, but the damage had already been done. I wouldn't trust another teacher again as long as I lived, and I know that they would never teach me anything.

I then sat the eleven-plus examination, which I narrowly failed, but because of the numerous days that I was unable to attend due to illness, I was given dispensation to repeat the year, my last in primary education. My father agreed with the educational authority to move me to Dunnikier, a school up the road. It was a non-denominational school, and believe me, I had no complaints about that decision.

Dunnikier School had a totally different atmosphere, and despite joining a well-established regime, I was easily accepted into the class. I quickly made friends with my classmates. One in particular, Roy Gibson, was to become a close companion of mine, and we were to share many experiences together.

My memory of Roy was of a blonde boy with a Perry Como hairstyle—all the rage at the time. His mother allowed him more individual expression than mine, and he was a real free spirit. There were others in the group, but Roy and I became constant companions. Despite my travels and adventures, he was more streetwise than me. His mother worked at John Menzies in the High Street—the shop where they sold all the records in Kirkcaldy. We would spend hours listening to the latest songs together. The sounds were wild and exciting, and I began to love the music.

Dunnikier School was so much better than St. Marie's. I progressed unspectacularly, but well enough to scrape a pass on my eleven-plus and gain entry to Kirkcaldy High School, where I was eventually expelled at the ripe old age of fifteen.

My father taught at St. Andrews, the local Catholic secondary school, so at least I was spared the indignity of being a teacher's son. I could think of nothing worse. My sister attended Kirkcaldy High School and was accepted by St. Andrews University. From my memory, she did so under some duress. Her choice would have been Edinburgh, but my father, for some reason, put pressure on her to accept the St. Andrews offer.

She had been popular at Kirkcaldy High School, especially with one of the male teachers, a fact that was to rebound on me during my brief spell at the school. Here was the brother of the girl who rejected his advances—I was at a disadvantage from day one. Eileen had also set the bar high academically. But for now, I could look forward to a summer holiday with some expectation.

Roy introduced me to my first paid job—a paper round. This didn't just give me spending money; it gave me access to the "girlie" magazines of the day. Parade was my favourite and featured some of the top models of that time, with Pamela Green and June Palmer as my favourites. By the time I delivered the publications to the shop's male customers, usually waiting impatiently by the door with a cup of tea in one hand and a cigarette in the other, some of them were so well leafed through that they had almost lost their structure.

"You wee bastard!" they would shout as I sped away on my bike, but I am sure they were too embarrassed to complain to the shop.

It was during that summer that Brian and I discovered golf. Almost daily, we would cycle down to Balwearie Golf Course. We would sometimes play two rounds a day and become fairly competent golfers. It was addictive, and for about six weeks, every waking hour was spent on the course. It kept us out of the house for long periods. Tensions in the house were worsening, and although our parents tried to conceal it from us, it was obvious that things weren't as they should be. Tony remained a delight and, I suppose, had inspired a temporary cessation of the hostilities, but with each passing day, the arguments became fiercer. It was awful to experience.

My mother was irritable, and my father was aloof. He was compiling a school dictionary for Blackie's, a Glasgow publisher, and didn't seem to have time for any of us. My sister's escape route was to St. Andrews University to study. Her boyfriend at the time had a sports car, and like all young men, wanted to demonstrate his prowess as a speedster. On a stretch of road between St. Andrews and Pittenweem, he sadly miscalculated the bend, hit the verge, did a couple of somersaults, and landed upside down.

Eileen escaped with shock and some severe bruising. I remember her arriving home from the hospital dazed, bruised, clothes awry, and looking like a sorry mess. Her boyfriend had to later leave the Air Force because he suffered blackouts as a result of that accident.

The Fife roads took another Stevenson casualty some months later. Dad set out on a journey to visit Eileen at St. Andrews and invited me to join him. There must have been something more attractive on offer at home because I opted not to go. That was a decision I would later regret. It's not that I had a death wish, but if I had travelled with my father that day, I might have saved him a lot of pain.

Spotting his wallet on the floor, he bent down to pick it up just as he was heading around a bend. The car wrapped itself around a lamppost and inflicted a lot of injuries on my poor father. If I had been with him, I surely would have picked up the wallet on his behalf, and he would have reached St. Andrews in one piece.

After the event, he looked like a soldier returning from a front-line battle. What a state! I think that was a few months before he ripped his Achilles tendon and ended up in an orthopaedic ward for what seemed like an eternity.

CHAPTER 15

Get a Job

Once my inhaler kicked in, I returned home after my final encounter with the head teacher of Kirkcaldy High School and was given an unexpectedly easy time by my parents.

"Well, Mike, said my dad. "If the idea of finding a place at another school disturbs you so much, start looking for a job." Fair enough, I thought—I will. But it was my burgeoning career as a local rock star that was foremost in my mind. I was fronting a band called the Gravediggers, who gigged around local church halls and made the occasional foray into the Fife hinterlands, where I miraculously found myself the subject of adoring girls.

If only I could have shown my former head teacher how I came alive on stage. How I felt this almost overpowering surge of adrenalin and how my confidence would soar. I was transformed. My signature was to swing the microphone stand as though it were a Samurai sword and run around the stage in a theatrical frenzy. Our speakers were made in the shape of coffins to add mystery and menace to our performance. I was recognised and applauded when I took the stage.

I began to realise that sitting in those classrooms, my brain wasn't dysfunctional; I wasn't useless—I was alive with dreams and ideas. I saw a big world out there, full of endless possibilities. The teachers lived in a smaller world than the one I knew. I wasn't stupid; I was bored. Rather than being disinterested, I was desperate to learn and thirsted for inspiration.

In the 1960s, life at school was still based on the industrial model—a knowledge factory. I will argue till the day I die that teaching like this is fundamentally flawed. It demands complicity and obedience—neither was natural to me. I was a silent rebel. My role models by now were the Beatles, Rolling Stones, Pretty Things, The Who, Animals, and Yardbirds. They were challenging life as we knew it and creating sounds that excited me to my very core. These were pioneering times, and I wanted to be part of the revolution sweeping across Britain, America, and Europe.

The dullness of school life could never compete with the new ideas in art and music that were starting to imprint on 1960s cultural life.

My parents now allowed me more and more latitude because they were engrossed in their own problems. Their marriage was effectively over, and what was left of our family was hanging by a thread.

Eileen, my sister, had married and gone off to live in Zambia. I was just getting to know her husband Ian and was enjoying the company of my new brother-in-law. I had refused to see them off—so devastated had I been at their departure. I felt betrayed and abandoned. Thankfully, Eileen came in search of me as the taxi metre ticked away, and we embraced. I was distraught. The house had begun to feel like home, and having my big sister around meant so much. History was repeating itself—life at home was about to disintegrate. We had been apart before. When we went on a family summer holiday from Pakistan to Egypt, Eileen was asked if she would like to stay with my maternal grandmother and my aunt Clarisse and her husband Henri in Alexandria and attend school at Sacre Coeur for two years. She jumped at the chance, and we left her behind. We picked her up on our way back to Scotland.

I wasn't sure why my parents were so upset with one another; my first inkling came when I returned home one evening to find my mum sobbing. "What's wrong?" I asked. Oh, how I wish I hadn't. My world and any sense of security I had built around family and home were about to come crashing down around me. "Your dad", she said with quivering lips, "is having an affair with Lisa." "But Mum, she used to be dad's student and..." Before I could finish my sentence, I knew it was true.

Suddenly a picture emerged in perfect clarity—the private lessons, the babysitting gigs for Brian, Tony, and I... and the late return from school. It was horrible.

My parents had been my rock and my travel companions, sitting vigil by my bedside when an asthma attack would persist and always there at mealtime. I cried so much that night that I could have floated a yacht. Brian lay in the bed next to me. I didn't want to tell him and shatter his world. 'Lisa?' I couldn't take it in. She was only a few years older than me, for God's sake, and of legal age, but still! I couldn't sleep that night.

My thoughts returned to Pakistan and how safe I had felt with my parents amid the mayhem of Lahore. I remembered how I would grab at my father's shirt and snuggle against my mother as we walked through the bazaars.

My parents were everything to me, and at the moment, I would have done anything to heal the wound in their relationship. It wasn't going to happen and life at home slowly deteriorated from that point on.

Mum, Odette, was French-Lebanese—an intoxicating mix reflected in a rare beauty that she never allowed to slip away, even in her advancing years. She was born in the romantically named city of Zagazig, Egypt, and lived in Alexandria for most of her childhood.

She met my Scots-Irish dad, Jim, in a British Army club in Alexandria. He had fought in the desert campaign during the war, fallen in love with the Egyptian people, and taken up a teaching post in Alexandria while still in the army. They were both remarkable people, and I wanted them to be there for me together forever. They had given me both life and a love of life's fruits.

The memories were vivid and fast-coming.

I remembered that day at Pakistan's Murray Hills when, while playing a solitary game close to a railing that lined the edge of the precipice of a thirty-foot drop, my mother screamed at me to move away from the danger. That was my signal to defy her instructions. Moments later, as I performed acrobatics on the railings, I lost my grip and went into free fall. Fortunately, I hit an unsuspecting cow on the way down, which broke my fall and minimised my injuries. Not so for my father, who, out of paternal impulse, raced to the scene, leapt over the railing, and jumped the full drop onto a rocky verge littered with sharp stones and broken glass.

I remembered the horrible day when, out with my dad in Lahore, he suddenly and inexplicably fell to the ground, convulsing. I was alone with him, terrified, and rooted to the spot. "Dad, Dad, please stop", I whimpered. It seemed like a lifetime before nature restored him. His lips were bloodied, his head was covered in dust, and his voice was groggy. I had him back, and that's all that mattered. I held him so tightly at that moment.

I would find out later that it was epilepsy.

I could smell and taste the meals my mum had prepared—she had given me a love of food, colour, style, and theatre. I remembered being taken each day to kindergarten in Lahore with a tin containing curry, chapattis, and a glass of lassi. I remembered being mesmerised by the backstage activity of an amateur drama production she took part in—as the only female character in a cast of young Pakistani men.

Those years swept before me in vivid pictures.

When you move from place to place, bricks and mortar are merely staging posts. Home is the people you are closest to—family—and that was being ripped from me. I was inconsolable. Perhaps all of that had contributed to my disinterest at school, but on the day I left for good, I felt a surge of enthusiasm about the adventure ahead.

Getting a job was easier than I thought. Walking along Kirkcaldy High Street, I spotted a vacancy sign in the window of Neville Reed, the tailor. I went in, inquired, and took part in a short interview—part of it puzzlingly focused on how many girls I knew. It didn't take long to learn why this question was so critical to the job offer.

My dad bought me a suit, and I started on the following Monday. In those days, men's tailoring shops were ubiquitous: John Collier, Burtons, Neville Reed, Hepworth's, Jackson's, and Dunne's. Most of these existed cheek by cheek in Kirkcaldy High Street.

The High Street was abuzz with shops and life in those days, hosting two of the town's five cinemas and a whole host of small independent shops.

My first job at work was to brush off the dust gathered on the ready-made suits that hung around the shop. It was a tedious and seemingly endless task that simply served to recycle the dust and trigger my asthma.

I learned a few dodgy sales techniques—the worst was to tell a customer that the suit fitted them like a lord, even though the trousers trailed hideously below their testicular area and the jacket dwarfed them. I learned how to measure men up for a bespoke suit and ask that excruciating question: "On which side do you dress, sir?" Perhaps Fife wasn't the most sophisticated cultural centre because, invariably, you would have to explain in more earthy terms. "Your penis, sir, on which side?" So nervous was I at my first attempt to measure an inside leg that I thrust the long end of the tape measure too far and too fast in an upward direction that I almost ended this poor man's ability to dress on any side.

As my confidence grew, I would stand in the doorway with my hands behind my back, waiting to chat up potential customers with subtle words of engagement. "You have a beautiful wife, sir." That one worked well, and it also prompted a few witty ripostes: "I'll leave her here for you then." or "Do you not need glasses, lad?" We have come a long way in sexual politics since then.

Within a few weeks, the girls started to gather at the front door of the shop. This was much to the delight of the manager, who made me an offer I found *easy to refuse*. "Get them to come upstairs, and you and I can—you know?" On my fourth refusal, he sacked me for insubordination. I was aggrieved but relieved.

CHAPTER 16

The Band

Singing in the band was taking up more and more time; my hair was beginning to creep over my ears, and I seemed to have the wingspan of an albatross. I began to 'look the part'. My hair's natural instinct was to curl, so it took longer to grow than I had hoped, and then I read somewhere that it was possible to iron your hair straight. Excited by this discovery, I decided to make the transformation that night. I used brown paper to avoid singeing my hair and did everything by the book—except the angle at which I placed my locks on the ironing board. The result was certainly straighter hair, but it stuck out like a candelabra from my head—a greased-down rock star look it wasn't.

The next day, my hair was washed and dried back to normal, and we gigged at my brother's school. Standing on a flatbed truck with the whole school in attendance, I felt on top of the world, especially seeing Brian take pride in his big brother. His chest swelled that day, and I am sure his stock rose at school with the students—not so much with the teachers.

On stage, I didn't care.

I was nerveless, and my front man antics were getting wilder with each performance—it seemed I was firing up other members of the band, and in Dunfermline two days later, they decided to mimic The Who, smashing the speakers and guitars. Unlike Pete Townsend and Keith Moon, we could not afford the replacements.

What you learn as a performer is that you have to be distinctive.

I was daring to be different—I was far from a great singer, but I put on a unique show. When the Sensational Alex Harvey Band played in Edinburgh in the early 70s, I was thrust onto the stage by Brian and his friend Paul in answer to a call for unusual talent.

I stripped to the waist and drank a can of beer while simultaneously flexing my arm muscles and rolling my stomach like a seasoned belly dancer. Daft as a brush, but Alex Harvey, a large enthusiastic audience, and The Kinks watching from sidestage loved it. For months afterwards, I was asked to repeat that performance in bars throughout the city, earning free pints of beer in the process. This was the same talent for performance that I had shown at school and been belted for.

In the 1960s, we were lucky to have a new YMCA building that attracted some of the most celebrated bands around. John Mayall's Blues Breakers, Taste, Robert Plant (later of Led Zeppelin), and his Band of Joy were among my favourites—add to the mix great Scottish bands like Marmalade, The Beatstalkers, Dream Police, and Studio Six. We were rarely without top entertainment—even in a small town like Kirkcaldy.

What really excited me were the acts that combined music with theatre. Since my early years, I've had a love of the unexpected—I think my experience in other countries has fuelled that passion: wandering along the harborside in Naples with its sparkling jewellery shops and its singing waiters; the snake charmers in Pakistan; the children of Port Said who would ask you to fling a coin into the Suez Canal and then dive to retrieve it. There were also the colours, sounds, and scents of the Catholic Mass we attended—

these had all created in me a sense of 'life as theatre'. In Pakistan, Brian and I would dress as bishops, using a colourful garment as a cloak and a long stick for a mitre. We enjoyed organising mock services.

The desire to perform was evident in my early years, but over time, that passion slowly chipped away at home and at school. Our band changed all of that. It was like a veil had been lifted—a flowering of hidden desire. In my life, I have felt like an outsider. Now it was my strength, and this quality was firing my creativity. I was amazed at how different I was, and no longer shy. I have met so many people who have shared my experiences and were cowed by them.

Early creative characteristics are often identified in pejorative terms—from disruptive to nuisance.

Yet it is disruptive people who have always and will always challenge and change the world. New ideas come from those who have learned never to accept that 'what is should be'.

How often have you asked yourself: 'Why don't they____?' or 'What if____?' You've seen the blindingly obvious, so 'why haven't others?' You will recall observations you made years ago coming to pass. Yet your voice was never heard. And who would listen to you anyway? You sit on the sidelines, watching one car crash after another.

How long was apartheid allowed to continue in South Africa? For many years, the British government didn't challenge it, and the Prime Minister regularly referred to Nelson Mandela as a terrorist. In Montgomery, Alabama, inspired by Martin Luther King to take on the fight for racial equality, Rosa Parks refused to obey a bus driver's order to give up her seat to a white passenger and was arrested.

World history would have been redrawn if these great icons of change hadn't stood up and challenged the way things were. Closer to home, would every organisation still use garbled tomes (gobbledygook) in customer communications? What if Chrissie Mahler, a feisty Liverpudlian, hadn't said, "Enough is enough", and set up the Plain English Campaign? She has since helped clarify everything from tax forms to bus timetables. She wasn't the first to observe that what she read made no sense to her, and yet she didn't assume that the problem was her lack of comprehension. With that lens, Chrissie was able to retain the ability to see and challenge the absurd.

I am confident about challenging the status quo and speaking out. That confidence doesn't come from some great epiphany in my adult life; it comes from secondary school, where I gave up trying to fit in and began to discover my authentic self. With so much pressure around us to conform, it is easy to believe that we have to join a club, a movement, a political party, or a gang in order to be accepted.

The real courage is in retaining our own beliefs and ideas and standing up for them. In any sphere of life, it is those people who fiercely defend their individuality that we secretly admire—from Lady Gaga and David Bowie in rock music to Denis Skinner and Tony Benn in politics. They cannot be easily classified because they stand outside of convention.

So often, we shake off that ability to see the abundantly obvious and ask clarifying questions. We want our young people to accept the world as it is. We narrow rather than expand their horizons and presume to manage their expectations. Then we compound the misery and uncertainty of youth by telling them, "These are the best days of your life." I was told this repeatedly. There I was about to start my adult life at fifteen—hormones out of control, spots on my face, ears that could span a river, regularly beaten up by a gang, parents warring at home, and then deemed a spectacular failure at school.

Amidst all that adolescent angst, I had been taught to expect life to spiral downward. What a joke. When I speak to young people, I dispel that notion. "The best is yet to come," I tell them. You can see the pressure lifting from their already overburdened shoulders.

It is so easy to lose a sense of who we really are. The influence of parents, teachers, siblings, peers, partners, workplace colleagues, the media, and the emotional impacts brought about by major incidents all conspire to shape our personalities and behaviours. We are urged to conform and accept.

As a motivational speaker, I meet many people who know they underachieve but don't know what to do about it.

They have lost sight of who they really are.

CHAPTER 17

Job Search

My search for another job got a sudden boost when my friend Elizabeth mentioned that her father managed the furniture department at The Co-op, where members got dividends as a share of the profits. "Why don't you ask him for a job?" she said. 'Furniture sounds fun,' I thought, and the next day I went to speak to Elizabeth's dad—he had obviously been prepped for the meeting. He was lovely and offered me a job on the spot. What I liked about The Co-op was the vast variety of goods it sold—from perfume to carpets. There were four floors, and I was stationed on the top floor in an emporium of sofas, wardrobes, nested tables, dining suites, and beds—and in one corner, a colourful array of carpets.

It was a five-minute walk from home, and I knew Tom, a rival singer who worked in another department. There were lots of girls to admire, working or shopping, and I wouldn't be asked to supply girls to the manager—because Mr. Dunsyre was far too decent for that. Plus, my weekly wage was to rise by 5 shillings to £4 a week.

As I surveyed my new empire, I was introduced to my colleagues, Mr. Smart and Moira. Mr. Smart, a small and immaculately dressed man in his 90s, was a great wee character from whom I learned so much. Age is only what we allow it to be. Moira was a down-to-earth

Fifer who seemed to find everything I said funny—they both took me under their wing.

On my second day, I met Tom for a sandwich. His band was doing really well around Fife. "Why don't you get some clothes made-to-measure?" Tom suggested. "You can decide on material and style."

I took Tom up on his suggestion and had a pair of pants made as well as a green doeskin regency styled jacket. The Harris Tweed hipsters were a clear mistake. With limited lining, it was like rubbing steel wool repeatedly against my genitals. As I walked to my gig, I tried to adjust my stride, but that only served to make me look like an even bigger idiot—just the excuse my tormentors were looking for as I rounded the corner into Kirk Wynd, and there they were—Paddy, Eddie, et al. Their hobby was to beat me up and leave me for the crows—something they did repeatedly. First, there was laughter. "What the fuck are those?" "My new trousers," I replied. Then came the assault—boots and fists raining in on me with the occasional comment, "Poof," a pejorative term for homosexuals. I was used to this by now and was able to time their assault to the nearest second. Only two kicks to go. I was right. Off they went in search of their next victim, leaving me bloodied and bruised and my new specially commissioned Harris Tweed trousers in tatters.

Music, more than anything, had helped to build my confidence, and I found that I came alive on stage. I felt a massive surge of adrenalin standing in front of an audience, and when I began to sing, it seemed that my personality was transformed. My signature action was to swing the microphone stand around my head and run around the stage in a frenzy.

I was very aware of the theatrical value of live performance, putting on a visual show, and creating rapport with the audience. Like The Who, I'd prance on stage, kicking over amps and speakers. I was recognised and applauded when I took to the stage, and I began to realise that my brain wasn't dysfunctional and useless—I was alive with ideas. I saw that there was a big world out there full of endless possibilities. The teachers lived in a smaller world than the one I knew. I wasn't stupid; I was bored rather than disinterested. I was keen to learn and thirsted for inspiration, and music was the first thing that provided that.

CHAPTER 18

The Bullies

My newfound status as a rock star, however, made me more of a target for the bullies in my life. I was victimised by these lads, as they beat me up habitually with unfailing brio. They were the same age as me and about as academically inclined. They weren't much bigger than I was, and if I'd been pitted against them individually, I most likely could have held my own. But collectively, they were a force, and so from the age of twelve until I was fifteen, they terrorised me on a regular basis.

All of them came from homes that were poorer than mine. One was the son of a notorious petty criminal who was in and out of jail throughout our time at school. I suspect they resented me because of my parents' apparent elevated social standing. My father was a teacher, and my mother was a well-known member of the town's genteel sorority, which would now be termed 'ladies who lunch'.

Undoubtedly, my tormentors regarded me as physically inferior, and the fact that I appeared to be on a similar career trajectory created in them feelings of anger. They picked their moments with cunning and precision to ensure they were never witnessed.

Invariably, they'd strike as I made my way home from school, but rarely at the same time or in the same location. The beatings were severe; I'd be punched repeatedly in the stomach, kidneys, and throat. My head was battered off walls, my shins were rammed with sticks, and my body was hit with rocks. When I collapsed in pain, I was kicked and stamped on. The beatings would last for up to five minutes, or until they became bored.

They rarely spoke, other than to deliver vile epithets as the blows rained down. No attempt was ever made to explain why they persisted with this ritual of violence. I suppose they thought the name-calling was enough clarification. My instinct initially was to resist, but with four against one, I soon realised it was futile and only prolonged the torture.

Attempts at supplication only made them angrier and more determined. After a while, I realised that lying silent and motionless during the beatings would create uncertainty and cause them to stop sooner. While I'm sure they suspected I was acting, they couldn't be sure, and so they'd stop kicking and punching, at least temporarily, while they deliberated what to do next.

Eventually, after a few days, my apparent lifelessness no longer seemed to matter to them, and they carried on regardless.

I never told my parents about the beatings because I knew that, even if they complained to the school and demanded action, nothing effective could be done to make it stop. I also feared the repercussions, not only from my tormentors but from others who would see me not as a victim but as grass. What motivated me above all else to do nothing and to allow the beatings to continue, day after day, was the shame I felt for allowing it to happen.

In the male-dominated, small-town society of the time, physical prowess mattered. To my young mind, seeking help from others would be an admission of weakness, which would be like admitting to not being a proper man. I can now see that my parents would undoubtedly have taken steps to stop it, but at the time I would have felt mortifying embarrassment. There had been moments of opportunity through the years when passers-by happened upon my beatings: neighbours, family friends, classmates' parents, or strangers stopped to break things up and the bullies would flee.

On each occasion, I would minimise the importance of what the bystanders had seen or thought they'd seen: it was nothing; we were just mucking about; I was as much to blame as them; I started it— and believe it or not, I'd manage to convince my would-be protectors.

By the age of fifteen, after years of beatings, I finally resolved to take matters into my own hands. For several nights, I was unable to sleep as I crafted a plan, worked out the logistical actions, and attempted to summon the courage to follow through with it. I was ready for the next inevitable assault to happen. I just didn't think it would happen that weekend, where I was forced to bring my plans forward.

Matters came to a head on Saturday morning as I wandered around the Links Market. It was, at the time, the largest and longest annual fair in the UK. The quartet of my tormentors appeared suddenly from around a corner. I figured they wouldn't act there and then in the middle of a busy market fairground packed with potential witnesses. Then, from the sneering grins on their faces, I knew instinctively what their plan would be.

Despite having planned Monday's encounter down to the finest detail, I knew at once that this was my best chance. Without stopping to think through the consequences, I walked purposefully towards them, staring each directly in the eyes. It was as though the years of torture and pain had emboldened me.

My arms seemed to be bigger and stronger, and my thighs were more powerful. In those few moments, I felt like I was surrounded by a protective shield, that even if they turned on me and showered me with punches and kicks as they always did, I wouldn't feel a thing.

Before I had time to think about what I might do, I was standing directly in front of them. Face to face with the ringleader and close enough to feel his breath. Without any warning, I sprang at him and rained punches on him. He staggered backward and crouched down, lowering his head into his cupped hands. As he did so, I brought my knee up and forcefully made contact with his face again. The other three backed away. Their faces bore the same expression of incomprehension. I swung my fist at one of them, intending to hit his face, but he backed away, and I missed.

I fully expected the others to jump on me and beat me senseless until the ringleader had recovered. Surprisingly, they continued to move in the opposite direction.

That was the last time I was ever beaten up by the bullies, and while I was glad, I no longer had to endure their relentless violence, I didn't feel good about the way it had ended. To this day that fight in the market in Kirkcaldy remains the only time in my life when I've ever instigated violence.

Standing up to those bullies and giving them a taste of what they'd dished out to me may have brought things to a head and ended the beatings, but the impact on me was longer-lasting and arguably more hurtful than the physical damage ever was.

CHAPTER 19

Cream

The other part of my bespoke purchases survived and helped me have one of the greatest nights of my life a year later, on a return visit from London. My green jacket was unique, and I felt like a Carnaby Street model in it. When news came that Cream were playing days later at the Kinema Ballroom in Dunfermline, I was ecstatic.

Cream was the first real supergroup and a monumental draw. The chance to see Eric Clapton, Ginger Baker, and Jack Bruce in the flesh was too good to miss. Brian and a coterie of his friends had arranged to go. "Great, I'll tag along," I said. "Sorry, Mike, but there's no room in the car." When I told my dad about my dilemma, he offered me an alternative. "I'm going to Edinburgh tomorrow afternoon and can drop you off in Dunfermline." With plans made, I allowed myself to get excited. Nothing could have prepared me for what was going to happen.

The next day, dressed in my signature green jacket and black trousers with their silk stripe, I set off in the family car with Dad at the steering wheel. It was hours before the concert was due to start, so I walked around the town centre, getting progressively closer to the Kinema Ballroom. Around 5 p.m. a transit van pulled up, and the window wound down. "Great jacket, man," said a very English voice. "Where did you get it?" "I had it specially made." "Wow," he said, "you wouldn't sell it to me, would you?" "Not a chance," I replied. I irrationally pulled it tightly around my chest. Accepting my answer, he asked if I would help them carry some equipment in through the stage door of the Kinema. It must be a backing band, I thought. Once I had agreed to help, I asked, "Who are you? Do you play in a band?" "I'm with some roadies for a band called Cream." "My god, I'm going to see them," I stuttered. "You're in luck, mate; you're getting in free." I was gobsmacked. Wait until I tell my friends about this.

The night was about to get even better, though. After helping the crew assemble all the kit on stage—a mammoth operation compared to my own band experience with our Vox AC30s and customised coffin speakers—Ginger Baker's drum kit alone was a major construction. All set and ready, we retired to a side room just as Eric, Jack, and Ginger walked through the door. "Nice jacket," said Jack Bruce. This was extraordinary. Here I was sharing a dressing room with my idols. They passed me a joint—the ultimate acceptance. "Let's have Mike stand guard by the front right stage speaker," suggested one of my new roadie pals. When Brian and his pals walked into the ballroom in the surge of the crowd, there I was, standing proudly on stage with my new responsibility as a Cream minder.

It was a fantastic moment as their jaws dropped to the floor.

At the end of the night, I was given Ginger Baker's customised drumsticks as a memento. The number of deep scars in them was a reflection of how much effort he had expended during the show. What a night! I was determined to widen my horizons.

Life at The Co-op was still good, and I was learning a great deal about the products, honing my sales skills, and making new friends. I especially loved that system, long gone, for sending the money through to the finance department in a brass capsule and getting a receipt and change delivered back to you. It worked by suction; it took moments, then it was a deal. In those days, cash was king, and most people paid with notes and coins.

At night, it was band practice or a performance. The line-up behind me had changed. Two highly experienced guitarists—one on rhythm and the other on lead—joined our band. They added new qualities, and while the raw edge had gone, we enjoyed a wider appeal—our fan base was growing.

I had a few girlfriends that year. When Norma arrived on the scene, I was mesmerised—she was a bit older and had a dangerously sexy air about her. She was a bit retro in her appearance—the high heels, the half beehive, and the hugging dresses. We dated a few times and were getting really close. Then, out of the blue, came a bombshell. At the YMCA, someone came up to me and whispered in my ear. "You're a dead man, Stevenson. Do you know you're going out with Muck's girlfriend, and when he returns, he will take you apart limb from limb?" Muck was apparently a deep-sea fisherman with a violent and possessive streak and was due to return from his latest stint in two weeks.

Oops. Perhaps London was closer than I thought.

I had to end the relationship with Norma, and I did so with a heavy heart. She was beautiful and she had a sense of sophistication about her that I adored. She was tearful and told me of her intention to leave Muck. 'Jesus,' I thought—that's worse. I can't imagine Muck giving us his blessing. I was a dead man walking.

Now was surely the time to make the move to London.

I was almost sixteen and ready to spread my wings beyond the small-town confines of Kirkcaldy. I was still an eight-stone weakling but confident that I could make it in London.

That night I told my mum and dad.

The conversation at least got them into the same room for a few moments. "Okay," said my dad, "but will you at least stay with Aunt Alison for a few weeks first?" Dad's sister and her family lived outside London, and yet it seemed like a reasonable condition. One phone call later, and I was ready to go. I said goodbye to the band members, The Co-op, my closest friends, and Kirkcaldy—home for the past five years. I could now put school, warring parents, random assaults, murderous boyfriends, and the constant smell of linseed oil behind me. There was sadness, too. I would be leaving my brothers, Brian and Tony, behind.

Tony had been born only five years earlier. When he arrived home in my mother's arms, our excitement was palpable. Brian would finally be a big brother. I remember hoping that Tony wouldn't suffer the pain of childhood that I had experienced, and I saw myself as the custodian of his welfare. He was too young to make sense of anything, but I would whisper to him how I was going to look after him, and he looked as if he appreciated my concern. Nothing I could do, however, would shield him from the breakup of my parents, and he was to suffer more than any of us in the long term.

Brian and I, despite the frequent fights, had never been apart and were closer than either of us would have acknowledged at the time. Then, of course, Mum and Dad—they had given me so much and yet taken so much away from me. My emotions were mashed up around them. They were on the brink of breaking up, and news of my dad's affair had spread beyond the confines of home and school—he had been forced to leave his job and now held a post at the University of Edinburgh, coincidentally where Liz had just been enrolled.

Kirkcaldy had been our most stable base yet, and I had dared to believe that it would one day provide a warm and cosy nest I could return to in years to come. I had made lots of friends and left some kind of imprint on the town—not least in providing regular practice for the town's thugs.

CHAPTER 20

Our Travels

Leaving home made me reflect on the last time I packed my prized possessions and said farewell. It had been nine years since we had left Pakistan, and as I retraced those years, I had an overwhelming sense of having lived through a fictional adventure. Leaving Lahore had been a wrench. A combination of my ill health and the fact that we had been separated from Eileen for so long caused my parents to rethink, and we plotted our journey back to Scotland. I remember my father showing Brian and me an atlas and explaining in detail how our journey was to unfold.

We would sail on an ocean liner to Port Said in Egypt, where we would stay awhile, pick up my sister, and then sail on to Naples in Italy. From there, we would go to Rome and then, by train over the Alps to Paris. The rest of the journey was straightforward.

When we said our goodbyes, it was off to Karachi, from where we would embark on our long journey homeward.

There is nothing like an Asian city at the height of its activity: the beggars, the strain of snake charmers, the oxen being driven through the crowds, the heat, the dust, and the frenetic activity around you are mesmerising.

Sometimes you feel like your head is going to burst with all the activity.

The ship we sailed on was called the Asia, and it was as huge as I was small. One or two incidents stick out from that journey. My enthusiasm for attempting to defy the constraints of railings and gravity was revisited when I manoeuvred my body over the side of the ship so that I could call to my parents and shout, "Dad, Mum look where I am." Thankfully, a steward, a no-nonsense Scot, spotted me and, in one sweeping movement, drew me back on to the deck and administered a swift punishment. There was no political correctness in those days.

Even that didn't teach me a lesson, as later adventures were to prove.

At Port Said, we were greeted by a different kind of energy—a military presence. British soldiers with fixed bayonets in hand strolled up and down the port. This was shortly before the Suez Crisis, and the British were still a major colonial power in Egypt. The Egyptian president, Nasser, had other ideas, however. He saw no reason why the Egyptians should continue to play a subordinate role to the British. Who can argue with that assertion? But at that time, the British fiercely guarded their power across the world. Egypt was about to slip from their grasp, and this was a tense time in the country. I was frightened to see the soldiers, but they didn't really impact our stay in the country.

I fondly remember my uncle Micho in Egypt, a handsome man who was very warm and hospitable. Regrettably, he was to die at an absurdly young age and deny me the opportunity to get to know him in future years. I suspect he remembered me for all the wrong reasons.

Having acclimatised to this new environment, it didn't take long to get back into my mischievous ways. Somehow, I had contrived to crash his beloved car. It was a beautiful black Citroen with side runners. I manoeuvred my six-year-old body into the driver's seat and released the handbrake. The damage would have been minimal if the car had been on level ground, but it was parked on a steep incline. The beleaguered vehicle and I rolled down the hill. Yippee! It was exhilarating. If not for a large, imposing tree, my first journey as a driver might have been considerably longer and more treacherous. Luckily, we were in the Middle East, and Uncle Micho saw the funny side of things, so the incident passed into folklore.

The journey homeward took in Naples and its magical array of port-side jewellery shops. Exquisitely crafted ballerinas danced around on music boxes; diamond brooches sat in velvet-lined displays; and amber, ruby, and emerald stones glittered in lit window displays. Later that evening, we went for a meal at a roadside restaurant. Checked tablecloths, well-waxed candles, a plateful of pasta, a bowl of side salad—it was like sitting inside a painting. Then there was the ample frame and imposing voice of a live opera singer.

Italy was an introduction to style. After the poverty and minimalism of Pakistan, we entered the European design culture. The sounds and shapes were detailed and beautiful. People ate and drank plentifully. There was no apparent poverty or struggle. People seemed to enjoy life to the fullest. Music and laughter filled the air. Shops and restaurants were alive well into the night. The smell of olive oil and garlic permeated the atmosphere, and there was character around every corner.

In Rome, we visited the Vatican and St. Peter's Cathedral, with their magnificent, imposing architecture and Michelangelo's finest creations. For a small child it was simply too much to take in. We attended a benediction in the cathedral led by Pope Pius. Embarrassingly for my parents, as we had settled near the front of this vast cathedral, the Pope finished performing the service and I cried out, "I need a wee-wee." I was quickly escorted down the seemingly endless aisle to the back of the cathedral by my red-faced father.

So far in my life, I have witnessed the reign of five popes and seen two of them in the flesh.

From Rome, we set off on a train journey through the Alps of northern Italy, Switzerland, and France—what an awesome sight that was!

I could remember nothing of life in Scotland, and no amount of parental guidance could have prepared me for the culture shock that I was to experience. We stayed at first with my grandparents in a terraced house in Comiston, a prosperous rather than ostentatious area of Edinburgh. It was a stricter regime than I had been used to.

While I was free to roam around the house and gardens in Pakistan, I was now faced with rules.

CHAPTER 21

Culture Shock

I recall arriving at my grandparents' home when our family got back from Pakistan. I found my grandmother quite fearsome. She was wiry, permanently attired in brown corduroys, and shrouded in the stench of cigarette smoke (I'm glad I inherited my sense of style from my mother), a symptom of that woodbine precariously perched on her lower lip. She came from a large Irish Catholic family and was one of only two children who hadn't pursued a career as a priest or nun. Between puffs she baked—I didn't think my digestive system had never experienced the stodginess of Scottish food; fried, baked, or just badly damaged, it wasn't what I had been used to during my global adventures.

My Mum told me that her first ever meal in Scotland after marrying my dad was 'potted heid' and spoke of the shock to her system. After a diet of freshly caught fish, chicken, rice, al dente vegetables, and an abundance of fresh fruit, her stomach must have done a few somersaults in those early days.

I was to suffer the sharpness of my grandmother's tongue on a number of occasions. It was a time of fear for Brian and me. Eileen fared better except on coal delivery day, when she took one look at the blackened faces of the coalmen and would scream and scuttle away to hide in a tiny room under the stairs.

Refuge for Brian and me was to be found in the back garden, which led to a small wooden bridge across a stream (or burn, as it is called in Scotland) and into a small stretch of woodland. We enjoyed our forays into the woods and had endless adventures on the bridge and among the brambles that grew upstream. It was a relief from the pressures of household politics and a welcome respite from the admonishments.

My grandfather, by complete contrast, was elegant and sartorial with a kind, sensitive, and measured demeanour. He avoided controversy, was impeccably mannered, and was in many ways a real Scottish Presbyterian. Honest and unblemished by pretension or anxiety, he worked in the medical service and was rewarded with an MBE for his contribution shortly before he died. His father had been a celebrated Lord Provost of Edinburgh and is recorded as one of the early movers in shaping plans for a road bridge across the River Forth.

The house was filled with tension.

My mother and my paternal grandmother would rarely see eye-to-eye, and there must have been many occasions when the atmosphere reached a boiling point. I felt sorry for my mum. What a contrast this must have been to her upbringing in Egypt. It was certainly an enormous relief to her when we moved into a top-floor flat in Leamington Terrace. That was to be our home for a couple of years. It had views across Bruntsfield Links on one side and a hotel on the other. I had never known life in the sky, but that is what it felt like. The highest I had ever had to climb was the stairs in my grandparents' home. This was markedly different, with four flights of steps and views across the city.

For the first few months, I was never away from the window. I would watch the window cleaners climb out onto the ledge, grip the window frame in one hand, and wash the panes of glass with the other. I admired them. They were always chirpy and whistled while they worked. They always had time for me as well. An encouraging pat on the head, a few incomprehensible words—it didn't matter. They were nice to me. They probably liked our house because of my mother, who, I imagine, fueled a few men's fantasies in those days.

One afternoon, having studied the techniques of a succession of window cleaners, I decided to save my mother some money. I went to the kitchen, filled a bucket of water, and with a rag in hand, I went to the front room. I opened the window, stepped out onto the ledge, made a few vain attempts to whistle, gripped the window, and leaned back, ready to complete my task. I achieved these first steps with such aplomb that my confidence grew and I started to hum. Eileen drew my mother's attention and as she entered the living room she froze. To this day, I will always admire her reaction. She didn't scream. She spoke calmly and softly, "Michael, I think you should come in now". By this time, I was cleaning the window with gusto, but I acceded to her request. 'Why not?' I thought. 'I have probably done enough. At least I have shown that a career as a window cleaner is a distinct option for future employment'.

I hadn't entertained the thought that one slip of the foot would have plunged me hundreds of feet onto the concrete below. Like all children, taking risks came naturally. The links opposite offered a safer haven for Brian and me. We would spend endless hours there. One of our favourite games was to emulate the Scottish rugby team, tackling each other and rolling about in the mud. It probably said much about the state of Scottish rugby at the time that we perceived success based on the degree of mud coverage we could achieve. The expanse of grassy hillocks, hollows, and knolls offered us an adventurous playground.

CHAPTER 22

A Day I Will Never Forget

Brian and I were enrolled to train as altar boys, and after mass each Sunday, we were kept back for tuition. I had never felt comfortable with the notion of devotion and was desperately seeking a good excuse to abandon the cassock and return to a career in window cleaning. I didn't have to wait too long, but I could have chosen a less painful way out.

It was at a time when my mother was visiting her family in Egypt, and I was feeling pretty vulnerable. I hated mum being away. I missed the reassuring hugs, the scent of her perfume, and her deft skills in the kitchen. We were brought up on the delights of Mediterranean cooking, and I always looked forward to mealtimes. I would consume anything my mum put on the table. I have always found eating well-prepared food a truly sensual experience. It all started in my mother's kitchen.

This particular Sunday, Brian and I had just completed our altar boy practice at St. Peter's Church in Morningside. Father Glancie saw us out into the church courtyard and laid his hand on my forehead with the parting words, "God bless you, Michael." He must have known something I didn't. Now feeling protected by his blessing, Brian and I set off on a short walk to the bus stop. First, we had to contemplate a zebra crossing (crosswalk). As we stood dutifully waiting to walk between the lines, a car stopped on the other side of the road and waved us across.

As I confidently set off, Brian uncharacteristically held back. "Come on, Brian", I shouted reassuringly as I looked back. Just at that moment, I was struck. The impact was fierce, and I felt myself being dragged for what seemed like hundreds of yards along the road. A motorbike with a sidecar had raced around the corner, ignored the crossing, caught my ear in his handbrake, and took me for an unscheduled, free ride down Morningside Road. I was hanging like a rabbit in a poacher's grip until he had the sense to release his hand from the brake and allow me to drop to the road. As he sped off into the distance, I lay in a state of semi-consciousness. My slender frame was badly battered and couldn't move. I thought I was dead, and I couldn't think with any clarity for a good-few-minutes.

My first coherent thought was for Brian, whom I had left standing at the side of the road.

The couple in the car across the road came to my rescue and lifted me into the back of their car. We were about to drive off when I saw Brian rooted to the spot where I had left him, and I screamed to my rescuers to collect him. The journey was a painful one, and I'll never forget the tears in my father's eyes when he saw the injuries. But children are resilient creatures, and after a few stitches, I was back for more.

Even at a very young age, my body had suffered countless blows, and curiously, I was beginning to enjoy the aftershock and perhaps the attention.

My asthma continued to dominate my childhood, and the doctor was a frequent visitor to the house. The relief after an attack is indescribable. One minute you are gasping for breath, and after a quick adrenaline injection, your body releases all the tension and you fall into a state of complete relaxation.

The needle held no fear for me, and by the time I reached my early twenties, I was like a pincushion. If I had drunk a gallon of water, it would have leaked as fast as I consumed it. I associated the syringe with the relief of pain. One of my parents would often have to sit by my bedside through the night and rub my back. It was the ultimate in security. It was the only time I enjoyed the close attention of my parents. At times like this, I never wanted them to leave me.

Nightmares and sleepless nights were regular occurrences in my childhood. I would lie awake for hours while innocent and familiar shapes became grotesque and threatening images. I saw giants bearing down on me, or my mind would wander into explorations that would leave me frightened and gasping for breath. I imagined the universe, its scale, and the insignificance of human presence in this vast open space. I tried to imagine how we came about and how we fit into the enormity of this planetary system. It would leave me exhausted in the morning, and at any excuse, I would feign illness to avoid school.

Now, at sixteen, I wanted to put all that behind me and start my new life in London. I was almost a free man, and I was ready, packed, and excited.

CHAPTER 23

London

I stepped down from the train into a noisy, frenetic, and soot-filled station. As I cut through swathes of disembarking passengers— some rushing to the exit gate, others taking stock of where they were and breathing in the putrid, smokey air—I spotted my cousin Adrian waving. He had been dispatched to pick me up. Adrian took my case and led me to his car, an Austin A34. He was taller than me, confident, urbane, and spoke with a polished accent. He was my father's sister's son. My uncle was in the Royal Air Force, so Adrian's family had lived in Malaya (Malaysia) and Ceylon (Singapore). He and his six siblings were all expected to do well and to go to university.

As we emerged into the hot sun, my green doeskin jacket was making me unbearably hot. Once in the car, we chatted about my reasons for the journey southward: job, money, and broadened horizons. I kept my rock star aspirations to myself.

The journey out of London was one from the throbbing heart of a busy city to the leafy and scented calm of Middlesex. On the Edgware Road, a small boy in a school uniform made his way onto a school bus. As it slowly moved off, he changed his mind. The bus stopped and released him. Adrian and I exchanged a smile—was that the timid child I had been in primary school? As we neared Bushy Heath, the landscape began to change—blossom-lined streets, large homes, and lush gardens. Here was wealth and privilege, a stark contrast to what I had left behind in Fife.

I was at first intimidated by meeting my aunt's husband and family—compared to my own family's unconventionality, they seemed so straight and high-achieving. I would later discover that they had precisely the same fragilities as we did. My arrival at their home couldn't have been more relaxed. "Hello Michael", said my aunt, mother of seven children. "You're just in time to help me cut the coupons off these cereal packets. As I was handed a pair of scissors, my eyes were drawn to a hideous sight sitting on the piano. It was a framed photograph of us, the Stevenson's, taken in a studio in Edinburgh years earlier. Mum and Dad were like bookends. Eileen had her surly look on while Brian and I were seated in the centre, grinning like Cheshire cats. All I could see were my ears. I had spent the last two years hiding them with my growing locks, and here they were in their full hideous glory. The photo was awful, and surely it was just taken out and dusted down for my arrival. It must have had them in stitches the evening before.

That evening, Adrian and his older sister Carol took me for a drink. Unlike at home, this involved a car. Amidst the tranquillity of an English country bar, I plotted my next step. I wanted to find a job. Adrian suggested I look in Watford because it was an easy reach from Bushey Heath. A few days later, I scoured the local papers, and one job leapt out at me: junior furniture salesman.

My interview took all of five-minutes, and I was in. Evidently, no one could understand my Fife brogue. A senior salesman named Geordie took me under his wing, providing an instant translation service and guiding me in the ways of life away from home.

The following day, Geordie said, "Why don't you move in with me?" In fact, he added, "Let's go for a drink after work and chat about it". We did that, and after a couple of beers, he made his intentions a bit clear. "You can sleep in my bed," he said, his hand firmly gripping my thigh. It was a pity it turned out like that. I liked him, but sexual relations with him were taking that affection a bit further than I wanted to go. Instead, I chose a bed and breakfast a few minutes-walk from the shop. My relationship at work with Geordie was a bit awkward the next day, and without his translation service, I would struggle in my sales role.

Now that no one understood my charms, I had become a bit of a liability to the shop, and my tenure was hanging by a thread. Selling a £50 suite of furniture for just £5 was the last straw; I had misread the label and lost the store £45. So, I was sacked just three weeks into my first job.

It was funny how just down the road a few weeks later, the customers seemed to not only understand me but would hang on my every word. This was my first experience with market positioning. Waring & Gillow customers expected cut-glass English to be spoken.

A short reprieve came in the form of a reassignment to the carpet fitting team; to be specific, I was to assist a seasoned fitter who sported a beard that was as oversized as his ego. "Oh, he told me, I have shagged so many women in this job." On our first day out, his charms seemed to fail him at our first stop, as the lady of the house shooed us away from the front entrance because we were tradesmen and that meant entry by the back door. Her tone was so contemptuous and dismissive that I wanted to argue. My new colleague's previously abundant sex life took a real plunge during our week together. Most of the women we met looked at us as though the cat had dragged us in. Later that week, I was told that my job at Warring & Gillow was to come to an abrupt end. But I had learned how to fit a carpet.

Next stop was Cawdell's, a department store down the road, where I was taken on in the linoleum and vinyl floor coverings department. Coming from the home of linoleum production proved an advantage—something I never thought I'd hear myself say. Part of the John Lewis Group, Cawdells was a whole different environment. This is where the less well-off people came to shop. I took to the place like a duck to water, and the customers took to me, in spite of my gnarled vowels and quirky sense of humour. I was really enjoying myself, and this time I was able to put into practise the full array of customer relations skills I had learned courtesy of Neville Reed, The Co-op, and Waring & Gillow.

It strikes me as extraordinary that, many years later, we still struggle with the notion of customer service. Being an egalitarian Scot probably gave me an enormous advantage. I saw service not as servitude but as a relationship of equals and a chance to make friends. Give great eye contact, a smile, and a couple of words to assure them that you are there for them; add a bit of well-placed humour; and avoid pressure sales—it works wonders. There aren't many jobs where you are given the chance to make people's day. That's how I saw this job, and I loved it. When a customer leaves the shop happy, your own spirits soar. I always advise young people to grab any chance they can get to interact with people. There is no better training for life.

An early discovery at Cawdells was a small cupboard behind the department that housed all the offcuts of vinyl and linoleum. Shortly after I found this treasure trove, a family arrived looking for vinyl for their kitchen and bathroom. They were so taken aback by the price they would have to pay that they were preparing to leave. They looked so despondent that an idea struck me. "If I could find you pieces from our stock of offcuts in a colour you like, perhaps I could sell you those at a reduced cost." They were interested, of course. Ten minutes later, they left with vinyl rolls in hand and a broad smile on their faces while I pocketed the proceeds. This was an easy scam. It didn't eat into useful stock; it benefited the hardworking and gave me funds to pursue my own interests.

Meanwhile, life at the bed and breakfast was getting tougher. First, I had to share my room with a builder from Cork, whose hygiene habits were suspect, and then came a Frenchman who spoke no English. We got by on my rudimentary French, but a real conversation never endured. Then came a group of Brummie pipefitters who had a month-long contract locally and who thought my accent was "foonay". Really? They would play three-card brag until the wee small hours and eventually I was forced to join in.

Breakfast was now my main meal of the day, and each morning I would be first to the table and last to leave—consuming every morsel of food available. The landlady and her husband took a special interest in me and served me increasingly lavish meals. At the same time, I was beginning to take a special interest in their beautiful daughter—this was to become my undoing in the weeks to come. They were a Jewish family, and their daughter was fiercely guarded from the guests. I would see her only fleetingly. She was like a rare jewel, and I started to fantasise about a relationship with her, but Mum and Dad had made it abundantly clear that she was off-limits.

With my extra earnings, I was now taking regular trips to London. I would shop at Carnaby Street and then go to the Marquee Club in Wardour Street, where I saw debuts by Yes, The Herd, Marmalade, and Dream Police. I met up with Hamish of Dream Police (later of the Average White Band) and members of Marmalade; it was great to be Scottish on those nights. On one such occasion, I missed my train back to Watford and so decided to wander the streets until early in the morning. At around 4 a.m., I was walking near Hyde Park when I met up with a group of three women and a guy. "Hi," they said in unison, and then, with a girl on each arm, I was dragooned into joining their adventure. They said, "Come to our flat and have some fun". They gave me a pill to help me get into the spirit of things, and within an hour, the world took on a wholly different complexion.

Their flat was spacious and well-heeled and taking it all in, I was overcome by a feeling of love towards my new friends. Taking a closer look at them, I saw their beauty and sophistication. "This is

Daddy's flat," she said, as she offered me a cup of tea. "He stays in the Bahamas for most of the year. "Come on," she said, taking her clothes off, "let's have a bath". Her body was so beautifully sculpted that I wanted to run my hands over it. She was like a porcelain figure. She grabbed me and started to undress me. "The water is hot. Let's go," she urged.

When we reached the bathroom, the other girls were already there, lying in a sea of bubbles. The guy was sitting cross-legged on the floor in his underpants, smoking a cigarette, and humming to himself. We bathed, listened to music, danced naked, and talked. When I left, it was five in the evening. I had completely lost track of time and missed a day at work. I had experienced my first acid trip, and I wanted more. I never saw these people again after that morning, but the rich eroticism of that experience will never be forgotten.

Back at Cawdells, I was forgiven for my unannounced absence and quickly re-immersed myself in the exhilaration of a life with linoleum and vinyl. It was business as usual; hard-up buyers would get offcuts for a knockdown price, and I would pocket the cash. Then one afternoon I was approached by a guy with short, cropped blond hair and a Crombie coat. I recognised him from a men's clothing shop around the corner. "Is it true that you used to sing in a band?" he asked. "Yes," I answered with a swelled chest. I saw this as an excuse to regale him with tales of rock stardom in Kirkcaldy. He seemed impressed and invited me to his band's rehearsal that evening. 'Why not?' I thought. 'This could be an entry point into my musical career in the South'.

It wasn't to be.

When I arrived that evening, the band was in full swing. I didn't like their music, but I offered some encouraging comments. Spotting my new white slip-on shoes, my new friend asked me if he could borrow them for a gig in St. Albans that weekend. I agreed and dropped them off the following morning. "I'll get them back to you on

Monday," he promised. That was the last I saw of the shoes, but it was far from the end of the story. On my fourth attempt to collect them, I saw red and pulled a penknife from my pocket and threatened to use it on him if he continued to retain my prized shoes. When I got back to Cawdells, the manager had received a call about my knife-wielding antics, and I was dismissed on the spot.

The next day I was walking down Watford High Street when, across the road, I spotted my shoe nemesis with a group of around twelve of his friends. I knew what was coming, and there was no way out, so I took the brazen path—crossing the road and greeting them like long-lost friends. They were momentarily taken aback, but soon the fists and the boots started piling in. Not a single part of my body escaped the blows, and the assault seemed to last endlessly. When they stopped, I got back up, and they started again. I kept doing this until they eventually gave up and moved on. I was beaten, but I remained unbowed. I flagged a taxi, but was refused entry to the car. "Don't want blood on the seats, mate," the driver said.

My next choice was as bizarre as anything I have done in my life. I walked into a cinema and bought a ticket for what turned out to be a weird black-and-white Japanese film. The girl at the ticket office looked aghast but said nothing. So, there I was sitting in a half-empty cinema, unable to see the screen without my glasses, covered in blood and bruises.

CHAPTER 24

The Streets of London

Returning to my bed and breakfast that day, it was the landlady's daughter who caught sight of me on the stairs. "Oh, my God," she said. "What happened to you?" Instead of giving her an answer, I asked her to sit with me. A few minutes later, she arrived at my door with a bowl of warm water and some cotton wool. Her tenderness reminded me of what I missed most about my mother's touch. Feeling tearful and in need of some affection, I pulled her towards me and kissed her on the cheek at the precise moment her mum walked in. "You must leave Michael," she shouted. Twenty minutes later, I left a tearful girl and my life in Watford forever.

After a brief resumption of family hostilities in Scotland, I returned to the heart of London. This time, a job and a place to stay proved more elusive. I had no choice but to take to the streets.

Sleeping out in winter is both cold and unforgiving, but you quickly learn the vascular system of a city. You see its underbelly—you see life in the empty streets as the detritus of each grimy, dusty day is cleared away. You begin to develop a sense of ownership for the streets you occupy and see early morning commuters as invaders of your space. You are a step ahead of them because you are living life in the raw and feel at one with the very foundation of humanity.

The streets are not a great place to sleep because you'll be kicked out of your slumber by a police boot. Hotel bins and heating ventilation grilles may feel hospitable, but they attract rats and cockroaches, which make unsavoury bedfellows.

I got to know Central London like the back of my hand—every nook and cranny. I was on speaking terms with some of the sex workers in Soho because we shared a sense of injustice. They would occasionally pass me a ten-shilling note while telling me I had gorgeous green eyes.

I had offers aplenty from men in flash cars trying to entice me to a warm bed and a nutritious meal. On the first such occasion, I found out too late that it was conditional. I was feeling particularly low and hungry that evening. The lights of the shops seemed to shine brighter than usual, the laughter was louder, and the smell of food was more intoxicating.

"You look as though you need a slap-up meal and a warm bed for the night." The voice came from the open window of a Jaguar. "Jump in." It was too good a chance to miss, so I did. I was taken to a house somewhere near Ilford, Essex. The house was full of activity when I arrived. There were around ten men and three women. I was told to undress and sit in the middle of the couch. There was no way of escape. I had started to fumble nervously with the buttons on my shirt when all hell broke loose. It was prompted by a telephone call. A shout went out, a safe in the corner of the room was thrust open, and three of the men, including my host, pulled out guns, put them in shotgun holsters, and ran out of the house.

The tyres screeched, and they were off.

Those left behind led me to a bedroom and told me to undress fully and get under the sheets. Terrified, I did what they said and stayed rooted in the bed for what seemed like hours. I must have fallen asleep from exhaustion because the next thing I remember is being told to get dressed and be ready to go. I was driven a few miles to a tube station somewhere in East London, given twenty quid, and told, under threat of death, not to mention the incident to anyone. I was utterly perplexed.

Later, I heard that the Evening Standard had carried the story of a hit in central London. That's all I can say about that, but the memory of that night will never fade. Men in big cars were now off the menu.

The homeless and dispossessed seemed to be drawn to me. I was beginning to emerge as a spokesman, able to articulate their wishes.

I ran into a friend from Kirkcaldy and found out that my parents had moved back to Edinburgh. The tensions between my parents had significantly worsened, and my mum was threatening a divorce. Who could blame her? I thought tearfully about my family and decided to return as well. It was during that stay in Edinburgh that I met the beautiful Sandy. She was sunbathing with her younger sister, Lorna, in Princes Street Gardens when our eyes met.

She was gorgeous—small-faced with blue eyes, a lightly freckled face, long golden hair, and slim legs. I wasted no time in making her acquaintance, and we soon hit it off. This unexpected turn of events prompted me to get a job, and I planned to make my stay more permanent. The next night I started as a dishwasher at The Wimpey Bar in Frederick Street, a cool hangout in those days. Sandy would meet me after work late at night, and we would court under the stars. She would make her escape from home through a bedroom window and arrive fragrant and smiling, while I stank of fat and dirty dishes.

Our nighttime liaisons were a breath of fresh air for me. We would lie in each other's arms in the gardens. It was while I was with Sandy that I met Duncan, another person I was immediately drawn to. Duncan had a worldly weariness that belied his young years—his eyes were bagged. I liked him a lot, and we had a shared vision of a better world in which we would both make our mark. When I wasn't with Sandy, Duncan and I would eat Black Bombers (speed pills) and talk endlessly about the possibilities that lay before us. I would be a famous rock star. He would be an impresario.

Weeks later, when Sandy's father found out about our nighttime adventures, he banned her from seeing me. I was gutted, and after a few unsuccessful attempts to circumnavigate the ban, I finally gave up. Sandy's promise that she would leave home and join me felt flimsy, and patience was not my strongest suit. Especially with London awaiting my return.

Duncan and I had become so close during these past weeks that it felt like a real wrench to leave him behind. He promised to make it down south soon.

Sadly, it never happened.

Four years later, I saw Duncan's face on a tabloid newspaper, alongside the awful news of his murder. The man arrested and charged I knew and loathed. Frank De Bere was a beast who tormented me on more than one occasion. He and his gang of thugs had raided a flat I was camped in. I was woken by a sharp poke to my ribs and a knife at my throat. Frank and his followers were looking down at me with their hideously smug grins. "Take the lot." Frank ordered them to scoop up everything they could find. I'd been scared witless. Now he was accused of stabbing my best friend more than thirty times. I was numb for days. Duncan dead? I couldn't take it in. It wasn't just his death, but the manner of it that preyed on my mind. Murdered by that bastard Frank.

I returned to London and ended up sleeping on a toilet seat in Piccadilly. I had reached rock bottom rather than rock stardom. Homeless, rootless, and hungry, I was celebrating a small victory. Having slept in parks, under bridges, and against hotel garbage bins, I had secured a cubicle in a toilet. Luxury, warmth, and safety were assured for at least one night. Each day had become about survival, and I was learning some valuable tricks. I knew when and which restaurants to go to for French bread sticks and fresh milk that would be left on the doorsteps. I knew how to navigate the Covent Garden fruit market for rich pickings.

Now seated in my new en-suite accommodation, I dared to look ahead.

There had been two attempts at finding me accommodation. Both had failed, but for very different reasons. The first was on a freezing night in December, when I was taken in a van to a large hostel, where I was told I would be fed, given a bed for the night, and then helped financially. It was the same humiliating experience I mentioned earlier. I had to strip and was hosed with delousing spray. I was then led to a dormitory that stank and was surrounded by the sounds of coughs, splutters, and angry outbursts. The next morning, true to what I had heard, I was interviewed by the social services and referred to a hostel for boys. I escaped at the first opportunity. The whole experience left me humiliated. I may have been homeless, but I deserved to be treated as a human being.

Why do so many of the services designed to help you, leave you feeling utterly devalued? When sleeping on the streets is a better option than entering a system to get you off those same streets, something is seriously wrong.

Even today, in business, there are those who think that leaving you to wait in some sterile, seated area makes them look important and in control. They could not be more wrong—the measure of greatness is how you treat people of all stations. I never keep people waiting, and I'm never too busy to have a word with anyone. When I hear the words "I'm too busy!" It infuriates me.

Never believe it.

There is a business saying that if you want something done, ask the person who has the busiest desk. People should always be valued as equals, and the great leaders that I have met make you feel ten feet tall—whatever your status. I love the story told by one of the Manchester United players when, after a really big game, in an effort to avoid the press, he took the low route out of Old Trafford. Deep in the bowels of the stadium, he spotted Sir Alex Ferguson sharing a cup of tea with a woman who worked the washing machines downstairs. He viewed her as an important team member and probably preferred her honest humility to some of the stuffed shirts in the directors' box. I subscribe to his egalitarian approach.

CHAPTER 25

Indiscretions of Cat

My second attempt at rehabilitation came when Marcus, a friend from Kirkcaldy, turned up at Piccadilly Circus one afternoon with two strikingly beautiful blonde women, Lil and Lottie. They were sharing a flat in Brixton and asked me to move in. One look at Lottie, and I was bewitched. She had the most penetrating green eyes, and I was utterly captivated by her. Marcus made it abundantly clear that Lottie was with him. It was a large bed arrangement, and although I was positioned between the two women, I was expected to turn my attention to Lil.

My breathing was laboured, and my attempts to avoid Lil's amorous attentions were making me increasingly uncomfortable. I was ready for the open air again, but my plans to leave were unexpectedly delayed.

The next day, Marcus announced that he was popping up to Grimsby for a couple of days. How could I leave two women alone in a flat? I decided to stay. That night, after a few more attempts to attract my attention in bed, Lil gave up and turned over to sleep. Then, just as she seemed to have dozed off, I felt a hand stroking my left thigh. It was Lottie. I couldn't believe it. I really fancied Lottie but had written off any chance that she could be attracted to me.

That night was glorious—we kissed, we explored each other's bodies, and we made love. We got a very frosty reception from Lil in the morning. Who could blame her for that? Lottie and I spent the day and that night together—it was lovely, but I knew it couldn't last.

When Marcus returned the following afternoon, Lil must have told him about our indiscretion. There was much wailing and beating of the fists before he performed his coup de grâce—putting his head in the oven. "Don't worry," Lottie said mockingly, "it's an electric oven."

It was time to move back onto the streets. I kissed Lottie goodbye and made a hasty exit.

Piccadilly Circus had now become the epicentre of my life, where I discovered 'speed' and 'acid' as a means to make life look and feel better.

Cat was my newly adopted name, so called because of my apparent similarity to Cat Stevens. Perhaps I was his doppelganger. Despite the rough sleeping, during the day I would stand under the statue of Eros like a Lord of the Manor. Night was a different story—a battle for shelter, space, and sleep. The drugs were given to me freely, and they made nights out in the open tolerable. A guy named Terry was a free source of speed, acid, and marijuana. In return, I would help him with his sales pitch. We learned that by employing our very different skills, we created a powerful combined force. He was a strikingly good-looking figure, and with his long, glowing golden locks and square jaw, he stood out in a busy crowd—while I could talk the hind legs off a donkey. Perhaps that lingering caress of the Blarney Stone when I was eleven was starting to pay dividends. I had become painfully thin, but my lack of physical presence was compensated by my ability to use words as a power tool.

It's in our cities where we meet people who alter our perception of life forever—one man, a Howard Hughes look-alike with a long beard and straggly grey hair, who spoke with eloquent pronunciation, held me captivated for a whole night. He told me how he had once been wealthy and successful, but when his wife and child died, he realised that he had lost the most important thing in his life. His pursuit of money had subverted his values, and he wanted to make up for that by eschewing all possession and property. It was he who, in my mind, distinguished the notion of home as an emotional rather than financial investment. His words resonate today more than ever.

He had made a choice and was happy with it.

He taught me that being true to what's important to you is vital to our sense of self and well-being. That we are seduced by material things, which will ultimately leave us without spirit or purpose. We spoke long into the night, and it drew out of me a desire to pursue language and music.

I later met a sixteen-year-old boy who had been persistently sexually and violently abused by his father and whose mother had hit him repeatedly and asked him to leave the house when he turned to her for support. His pain was etched in every expression of his being, and the last time I saw him, he had fallen prey to any man who would offer him a meal. It was his mother that I felt the most anger towards, because her denial was betrayal of the worst kind.

I met a girl in her late teens who, because she had done badly in her exams, had her food withdrawn until she apologised for damaging the family's reputation. She had been punished for her failures, yet if her parents had paid more attention, they might have heard her angelic voice and learned of her extraordinary ability to create words and songs out of her most profound experiences. Her talent was neither noticed nor valued at home. No wonder she preferred the honesty and integrity of a life on the streets.

Many had been thrown out of their family home or, like me, had found life so emotionally damaging at home that they felt they had to leave. Then there are those who have turned to alcohol and drugs. In the midst of the mosaic are stories to inspire even the most cynical among us. I discovered that resourcefulness exists in spades and that a wellspring of ingenuity and talent exists outside the narrow confines of academic life. The greatest among us are seared with scars and powerful stories. When you listen to stories of people's lived experiences there is so much to gain.

I met a man in his late forties who would craft beautiful models of some of London's most iconic buildings using any material he could lay his hand on: paper, wire, offcuts of wood, cardboard, tin cans, etc. He rarely spoke and would gather his materials at night and craft his exquisite mini-sculptures during the day.

John Muir, a Scot and the great father of environmentalism who set up the National Parks in America, was once a hobo. He saw life from the unique perspective of sleeping in the open air. He was a real visionary, and what he created helped save swaths of our natural environment.

My open-air sleeping experiences were exclusively urban, but I can imagine the enormous impact of living amidst the raw excitement of nature. As a child, nothing beats running through the woods, fishing from streams, climbing trees, and rolling down hills. Nature provides us with a veritable playground.

The relentless advance of unintelligent urban development has removed that opportunity from so many of our children. It is a crime for which the perpetrators will never be punished, yet the relationship between health, home, and environment is not a recent discovery.

John Muir said, "Everybody needs beauty—places to play in and pray in where nature may cheer and give strength to the body and soul alike." His biographer described his mission as "saving the American soul from total surrender to materialism." His intervention was critical to ensuring the preservation of nature at a time when every square mile of development threatened America's wild and wonderful terrain.

Look around our towns and cities and see what opportunities have been stripped from our lives. Green space is important for our mental and physical well-being. In London, I was beginning to enjoy the constant exposure to fresh air, and despite its obvious discomforts, going into a closed space made me feel claustrophobic.

I was beginning to learn that adversity could be our most powerful motivator.

Throughout my life, I have learned to find a spark somewhere to reignite my enthusiasm and step up to another level. The lower I have sunk, the higher I have stretched afterwards.

I was asked by students at a speaking event in Edinburgh what role 'fear' plays in leadership. I had to pause and think before I answered. To conquer fear, you must first acknowledge it and then stare it in the face. It has many expressions, some of which are ugly and destructive. I see bullying, heavy drinking, racism, and unprovoked violence as responses to fear. They are unconstructed and raw, like the fight-or-flight reaction of an animal.

Fear is within us all. It's an unavoidable human emotion. Yet it can be turned into something immeasurably positive.

When I say I focus on growth, learning, and continuous advancement to keep driving me on to challenge after challenge, I recognise that the underlying motivator is a fear of returning to that time in my life when I was riven with a sense of worthlessness. This is what fear does if we don't harness it and work with its destructive schemes. When we turn that fear into a galvanising and positive force, we can achieve extraordinary things.

Our dialogue with ourselves should always have a positive focus.

When we don't forgive ourselves, and those we believe have harmed us, we share our lives with a monster that gnaws at us. Each new possibility becomes tainted by the past, and we magnetise the very things we are trying to avoid. I learned this in relationships. I expected them to fail and then precipitated their failure myself. My internal dialogue was saying, 'I don't deserve this. It's too good to be true, it will not work out.' By telling ourselves that, we invite it to happen. For years, I would be the ruin of every great opportunity that came my way.

When I think of the women I fancied—who were screaming for my attention but I didn't hear—I saw them as too good for me. I can recall the opportunities I didn't take as a performer because I saw them as too far of a stretch. I remember jobs in which I could have gone for advancement but chose to sabotage my chances.

We close off routes that are open to us because we believe it is better not to have tried than to fail. My realisation of this came late in life, but not too late to change my life immeasurably for the better. Age has no meaning unless we allow it to determine our fate. A life without falls is a life unchallenged and unlived. Benjamin Disraeli said, "Seeing much, suffering much, and studying much are the three pillars of learning."

If I were to sum up what I have learned, it's those incidents and relationships that upset us that become our gold nuggets. When we allow them to do so, we can turn what others might regard as a weakness into our greatest strength.

CHAPTER 26

Emergence of Inner Strength

In London, I was experiencing the slow emergence of an inner strength I had never realised before. My asthma was something I dealt with on my terms, although the attacks were less frequent than at home, I would be admitted to Charing Cross Hospital for a couple of days. It was against everything that I had been taught, but sleeping out and living on a diet of drugs and scraps of food seemed to be making me healthier and more resilient. I was experiencing a rush of confidence in my ability to live independently from the army of protectors that had crowded my childhood. Having your family doctor as a neighbour during your formative years was difficult. I had felt hemmed in and unable to breathe—both literally and metaphorically. Now I was strutting the streets of London by day and sleeping in its darkest folds by night.

At that time, something else was happening. As the war raged in Vietnam, there was growing anger about the USA's ultimately ill-fated involvement, especially among the younger generation. Opposition was being expressed angrily across the western world, and a new consensus was emerging—this was a generation born in the immediate aftermath of the Second World War that truly believed in a world of peace. What's more, it was developing a loud and powerful voice through song, literature, and art. There were underground magazines like International Times being sold on street corners that spoke of a completely different world view. Songwriters, actors, and performers were using the Vietnam War as a means to express their passion for a new paradigm.

Suddenly, the hippy movement got serious—this was not just a lifestyle choice but also a political movement. Piccadilly Circus had become an identifiable hub for London's hippy population and was drawing the increasing attention of foreign tourists, daytrippers, and international media.

And I was in the midst of it.

A Japanese filmmaker wanted me to play the guitar and sing after he was told of my talent. An assistant was dispatched to purchase an acoustic guitar, and it was thrust into my hands. I sang Donovan's "Catch the Wind".

Girls from London's suburbs would hang around, hoping to be noticed, and tourists would nervously snap away from a safe distance. In the space of a few months, I had become a figure of curiosity. Life was far from comfortable, but I felt like I was at the heart of something—a cultural awakening.

The drugs were creating in me a sense that anything was possible. I was meeting lots of new people, and my circle of friends was growing daily. Celeste, a French girl I met, told me of a squat she was sharing in North London. I agreed to travel back with her that night. Celeste's eyes were filled with enthusiasm, and her zest for life was utterly infectious. She was from Bordeaux and had been in London for three months. I loved her attitude towards life and wanted to embrace her sense of optimism and fun.

Celeste found me a small space on the floor, and as we relaxed into the evening, three men who introduced themselves as Nick, Pat, and Fergus interrupted our conversation. Nick was Lebanese, while Pat and Fergus were, unsurprisingly, Irish. Lebanese and Irish? I couldn't believe my luck. The conversation flowed through the night, and my first stay in a squat ended without sleep. In the morning, Celeste and I joined the band of three and headed to Kensington Antique Market, which I imagined would be a dusty old warehouse run by old men in waistcoats.

I was wrong. What I found was a patchouli-scented three-story emporium selling hippy fashion, hairstyles, body arts, crafts, and accessories. The atmosphere was calm yet busy—beautiful women seemed to glide effortlessly in their long, flowing kaftans. Not since my early days in Pakistan, have I experienced such a variety of colours, fabrics, and scents. There were joss sticks, smoking pipes, Afghan coats, jewellery, and perfumed oils. Hookahs sat alongside silk scarves.

One stallholder beckoned me over and gently rubbed sweet-smelling oil on my forehead. The mere touch of her fingers on my skin had an immediate and intoxicating effect on me. I realised then how tense and physically isolated I had become. Human touch is powerful, and I was suddenly acutely aware of its recent absence from my life.

I learned a lesson that day that has stayed with me ever since. Even in a culture that is not intuitively tactile, we attempt to communicate with eye contact, gestures, and touch—even if it's just a light brush of the arm. It reduces space between individuals and makes a strong, reassuring connection. I didn't remember much physical contact with my parents—aside from those asthma attacks where a rub of my back would give me some relief.

Perhaps the asthma had become my cry for emotional and physical attention. Here at Kensington Antique Market, I was among beautiful, gentle people who were unafraid to express their affection with a light kiss or a full embrace.

Celeste, sensing my attraction to this girl, held my arm and guided me forward. The atmosphere of love and peace was clearly infectious—a few steps later, she stopped, pulled me close to her, and planted a kiss on my lips. I hadn't dared dream that this gorgeous and sensual French woman would find me the least bit attractive. Now here she was, in a close embrace. "Mike, you have beautiful eyes, and if you learn to use them, you will seduce any woman you meet. But please, not yet." I held her tightly and kissed her with such force that she had to push me off. "Slowly, Mike," she whispered; I was going to learn from this girl. Nicky, Fergus, and Pat had by this time left us to it, promising to meet up at the squat that night. Celeste and I wandered around the market for hours before making our way back to Piccadilly Circus. As the strain and pain of the previous months began to evaporate, Celeste took control of the tempo and mood.

I was being carried along by a wave of enthusiasm I had never experienced. Nothing was a problem to Celeste—only a small challenge to be overcome. I told her I was hungry. "No problem," she said, stopping a man in a business suit. "Please, Monsieur, I am so hungry. I haven't eaten for days, and I am weak." I was expecting the usual brush-off, but Celeste's seductive and pleading eyes had worked. He plucked from his pocket a five-pound note and gave it to her. Just like that. It was extraordinary. A whole £5 to spend. This was more than I used to earn in a week.

We found a small Italian restaurant and ate until our stomachs could take no more. I had found a girlfriend who had already changed my life for the better. I had not eaten a sit-down meal for almost a year and was so full I could barely walk.

Belsize Park was abuzz with lively conversation when we returned later that evening—there were two new additions to our group. Tosh was from Dublin, and Zack was from Liverpool. They were clearly plotting something out of earshot. That night, Celeste and I slept soundly in each other's arms.

A pull of my arm woke me. It was Nick. "We need you," he said, pulling me into the next room. Tosh, who was holding court, had a plan, and if I wanted in on it, I was to join them. He knew of someone looking for a large consignment of cannabis and willing to pay £2,000. Tosh was eloquent and highly persuasive, so when he said he would pose as the negotiator and negotiate the deal, there were no dissenters. This was a man with enough Irish charm to sell a Tory policy to a Marxist. "Where will we get that amount of gear?" I asked. The looks I got in return said it all. This was to be a scam. Feeling dumb, I felt I had some serious ground to make up and suddenly became animated with ideas.

Thankfully, Tosh and Zack liked my ideas, and I was taken onboard. The negotiation with this cash-rich buyer was to involve Tosh, Zack, and Nick. It was to take place at Kensington Antique Market, and if all went well, an arrangement would be made for the deal to take place a few days down the line. Fergus, Pat, and I would be there in the background until a deal had been struck. The next day, I was excited and nervous. Celeste, who had slept blissfully through the night, was unaware of our plans—because I was pledged to secrecy, she would have to stay in the dark. She sensed a change in me and asked me repeatedly why I was so highly strung. I wanted to tell her that in a few days, I could have a couple of hundred pounds in my pocket. More than I could have imagined in my wildest dreams.

Now I was faced with an additional challenge. I had arranged to meet the others at Kensington Antique Market, and I had to find a way to escape from Celeste. It was a measure of life on the streets. All I could think about was staging the attempted mugging of a passerby, knowing full well that the policeman standing a few yards away would give chase to me. Now that I was so familiar with the narrow, harrowed lanes around Soho, I knew I could outwit and outpace the men in blue. It worked, and aside from leaving a traumatised man and a bewildered Celeste, I made it to our meeting on time with minimal damage. Celeste wouldn't expect to see me until evening, so there would be no requirement for a lengthy discussion.

After a quick briefing, Tosh led our small delegation to the prearranged meeting spot and waited nervously for the arrival of their contacts. We watched from the sidelines, ready to leap into action if anything went wrong. The meeting began with an amicable shaking of hands. "It's a done deal," announced Tosh.

On Wednesday afternoon, he and Zack would meet them at Chalk Farm tube station and direct them to the squat, a prestigious north London address. "We'll have to be ready to spring the trap and make a quick getaway," explained Tosh. It sounded easy, but lots could still go wrong.

When I got back to Piccadilly, Celeste was surprisingly understanding about my earlier escapade, even if a bit troubled by my impulsiveness. Just as she began to relax in my company, I was spotted by a hot dog vendor whose mobile stall I had borrowed weeks earlier, made a few quid from, and dumped in an alley. "You bastard!" he screamed and gave chase. Twice in one day, I was in high demand.

Back at the squat that night, Celeste didn't return. I would never see her again. She was a remarkable woman, and I would have loved to have spent more time with her. Hiding my sorrow, I focused on my part in Wednesday's job. I was both nervous and excited.

When Tosh and Zack turned into the driveway with two smartly dressed men, one holding a briefcase, we were ready and waiting upstairs behind a door. Just a few more steps, just a few more seconds—it happened in a blur. I remember helping to grab one of the men and push him into an empty room. "Christ, he's got a gun!" shouted Zack, who was quick enough and strong enough to wrest it away from him. Now under control, Tosh ordered the men to remove their trousers, which he then threw out of the window.

The door had no inner handle, and we knew that their escape would take some time. "Right," shouted Fergus, "I've got the briefcase. Let's go." We raced down the stairs and out the front like greyhounds out of the starting gate. I don't know how I managed to keep up, but we seemed to have run for more than a mile before we reached the main road and jumped on a bus.

Breathless, silent, and shaky, we sat and stared at each other. We had done it. We found a bar in Swiss Cottage, and in the toilet, the proceeds were shared out. I had £200 in my pocket. This was more money than I had ever dreamed of having, and while we weren't shaken on the way back to the squat, we were talking to serious gangsters who saw us as an easy roll. We were targets, so we had to get away from London.

"What about Dublin?" suggested Pat. That was it. First, we needed somewhere to shelter for the next few hours. The Cromwellian Club seemed an unlikely choice, but we piled in there, flashing our wads of cash—our scruffiness was mistaken for that of a rock band. It's amazing what money does to the way people treat you. It's a nasty symptom of the hideously judgmental society we have created. After mingling with a few of the other guests, among them the Tremeloes, we enjoyed a few cocktails and sandwiches before ordering a taxi to the airport. I was saying goodbye to London, to life on the streets, and to persistent hunger.

I was on the cusp of a new adventure.

CHAPTER 27

Dublin Here I Come

I arrived in Ireland's capital to what you might call an auspicious welcome—slate grey skies, rain cascading down the street like a mountain river. Claps of thunder dwarfed the sound of air traffic. I stepped out of the terminal, and in moments I was drenched. "I am here," I whispered to myself. I should have been apprehensive, but I felt a fresh rush of exhilaration. I had escaped London and a gang that would surely now use every resource at its disposal to track us down. I searched my jacket pocket for a note of our meeting point. "Damn," it was sodden and the words were barely legible. First, I had to be confident about my destination. Soaked through, I returned to the terminal to dry it out over a heater. The words slowly re-emerged: Bailey's Bar on Duke Street.

"Where have you come from?", said my driver, howling with laughter. "London via Edinburgh." "Why didn't you take the direct route?" he asked. "Visiting family and all that," I replied. "There's nothing more fecking important than family," he replied. "My brothers are both in the Joy," he stated. "Joy? That sounds nice," I said. "The fecking prison. Mountjoy," he barked. That was the end of that conversation.

Before we had left Heathrow airport in London, Nick and I shopped for clothes there. I hadn't stepped inside a shop with intent for three years and felt awkward. Not Nick. He emerged from the changing room with jade green velvet trousers, a brown leather jacket, and knee-length boots. "Fuck," I said, "is that you keeping a low profile?" He was a 'flash guy' with his deep olive skin and broad white smile. He would have attracted female attention even without the peacock feathers that now adorned him. He'd been transformed from bum to international star in ten minutes. I opted for a more sober tan suede blouson jacket, black trousers, and a black shirt. Every mirror I passed, I had to take in my image—very cool. Just one day earlier, I was stuck in a squat in Belsize Park, sharing a dusty floor with an assortment of strangers. Before that, I had been sleeping on park benches or in toilet cubicles. This was literally an overnight change in fortune. I was determined to make the most of the opportunity.

In those first few weeks, we spent lavishly and were fast becoming a magnet for Dublin girls. They seemed to lack the inhibitions of the girls at home or in London. Catholicism does that to people. When you break out of its stranglehold, you do so wholeheartedly. I loved the chattiness of the Dublin girls and their willingness to embrace the absurd. They were always up for a laugh.

Spending each night in Fergus' mum's home was now getting a bit claustrophobic, and Pat had developed a nocturnal interest in me, which I was quick to discourage.

We found ourselves atop a flat above a bar. With our growing status as imposter rock talent scouts, we were approached by more and more wide-eyed aspirants looking for the big break. After a few weeks, the expensive lifestyle was beginning to catch up with us, and while our confidence was soaring, our financial wellbeing was plummeting.

While Tosh and Zack were establishing lucrative businesses, Nick and I were slowly retreating back into our previously impoverished existence. People here had taken to us, and we managed to make the seamless journey back into obscurity without being chased. Dublin is a city in which the unexpected is never far away. The city is full of characters, and every day you encounter something out of the ordinary.

With our funds ever diminishing, it was time to face up to the situation and think creatively about how to pay the rent on the flat and maintain our social standing. "Why don't you busk, Cat?" suggested Fergus. "There are no buskers with guitars in Dublin yet." It wasn't such a bad idea. I played a bit and sang. I was warming to the idea, and my growing enthusiasm was bolstered by Nick, who claimed to play bongos and could accompany me. "Jesus," said Fergus, "that would be dynamite. They would love that here". Over the next few days, we practised day and night. Now we were set for our first performance.

The first song I sang was "Hey Joe", quickly followed by "Not Fade Away" and "To Love Somebody". After our opening songs, I dared to survey the scene around us. It was extraordinary. We had drawn a large crowd, and people were even getting off the buses to get a closer look at our performance. Fergus was assigned to go around and collect the money, and while the coins trickled in, he lacked a real sales technique.

Out of the crowd came this shock of ginger hair. "Hoi lads, I'm Mary. Do you want me to collect for you?" Within twenty minutes, she had collected more than six pounds. Mary was a real force of nature—she swept in like a gale and took on the task of collecting cash with such gusto that no one dared resist her request. "These boys are fecking singing their hearts out for you," she would shout, "give us your money."

Thanks largely to Mary, we retired to the pub with more than £10, enough for Nick and I to take a performance fee and Mary and Fergus to share the reminder of the spoils.

Each day the crowds seemed to grow bigger and bigger, and we only needed to play two sessions to earn a good enough living. To put it into today's context, £10 is the equivalent of £150.

That night in Bailey's Bar, we were introduced to two local rock stars—Phil Lynott and Brian Downey, who had just formed a new band called Thin Lizzy. Phil, along with legendary Irish guitarist Gary Moore, had already achieved some success with Skid Row. The critics believed they were set to take the music scene by storm. The formation of Thin Lizzy was described by local music critics as a risk and probably doomed to failure. History, of course, was later to prove different.

Brian was warm, chatty, and curious, while Phil was far more aloof. A few years later, I was standing outside Wards Irish Bar in Piccadilly Circus when I heard my name being shouted. Here were Phil and Brian telling me about their first UK chart entry.

Moments like this stay forever etched in our memories.

Each day, our performances were getting stronger. To entertain an Irish, pedestrian audience, you have to offer a combination of musicianship and performance. You learn to project your voice and maximise the acoustic potential of the guitar. I didn't know it then, but this was the best training imaginable for so much of what has followed in my life since. The challenge of entertaining passersby and retaining their attention for a whole set is enormous. Yet that is precisely what Nick and I were doing.

My voice was getting stronger by the day, and our presence seemed to grow with each performance. This was 1968, and the only busker I saw around Grafton Street, now a centre for street entertainers, was an ageing blind fiddler with a small leather pouch attached to the end of the finger board—we used to swell his takings with some of our own as we returned each evening to our flat. I was also learning the art of storytelling. The Irish are great writers and talkers, with an unerring ability to turn even prosaic matters into great stories.

CHAPTER 28

The Troubles

In Londonderry and Belfast, there were stirrings. Catholics were treated poorly in the British-controlled North, and protest was growing ever more vocal and angry. The background to the anger was deeply rooted in history, and there was clear evidence that the big grievances were based on facts and not mere opinions. Even in Scotland at that time, you couldn't get a job in some of the banks if you were Catholic. Meanwhile, Northern Irish MP Bernadette Devlin, who was making a name for herself in the UK Parliament, was about to play a key role in the leadership of the Civil Rights movement. I admired her hugely as a politician because she was feisty, passionate, and utterly committed to her cause—in my view, a wholly just cause.

This was well before she slapped Home Secretary Reginald Maudling for his comment on Bloody Sunday in 1972. I was learning about Irish politics from some bright and passionate exponents, and I understood where the hatred of the British came from. I talked about the attitudes of British expats in Pakistan and seeing British troops in Egypt during the Suez Crisis. No one exemplified this passion more than Fergus' brother Pat, who was a veritable mine of information on Irish history and the injustices Irish people had faced.

My father would surely be proud of me, and news of his arrival in Dublin a few weeks later thrilled me. We had re-established contact, and I couldn't wait for him to see the new life I had carved out in Dublin.

Plus, I would be able to introduce him to my new girlfriend, Mhairi.

When Mhairi first appeared, her elfin face and big green eyes struck me. There was a wide-eyed innocence about her that I found refreshingly attractive. Rather than forcing her way into our company, she was shifting nervously about in the background. I went to her, and although shy at first, she soon warmed to the chance to chat. In fact, we lost ourselves in conversation that night, and hours later, we were hooked. She and I were to last for more than a few months in a relationship that would even continue back in Edinburgh. It felt good to have a regular girlfriend—and now with Mary and Mhairi, we had an even more formidable collection team when we busked.

Our notoriety as performers was getting us noticed. An Irish Times photographer turned up, and we were featured in the following day's edition. People would come from miles around to see us perform, and each night we had a choice of parties to attend.

Mhairi and I were getting closer and closer now, and in the truest Irish tradition, I was summoned to meet her family. The Cana Inn was chosen for the occasion. Little did I know that Mhairi was one of ten daughters. It was a daunting experience, and after the seemingly endless round of introductions, I was relieved to see Mhairi's dad shoo away my offer of a round of drinks and step up to the bar. It was like I had been surrounded by a whole set of Russian dolls—all the girls looked just like Mhairi but came in a full range of sizes.

As they giggled and stared, I felt like I was on exhibit. In truth, the family was lovely, and I was just beginning to feel at ease with it all when her dad announced a trip to the toilet, making it clear by his gesture that I was expected to tag along. "Are you planning to marry Mhairi?" he asked, as we both stood facing the urinal. "You've been going out for a good while now." 'For a whole fucking month', I wanted to shout. I feigned enough interest in the proposition to satisfy him.

Mhairi ended up marrying a friend of mine in Edinburgh a year later and went on to become a rich hotelier in the town of Oban.

My own father arrived in Dublin late one afternoon. Mhairi and I met him at the airport. He was clearly taken by Mhairi, and she by him. I was amazed at how confident and talkative she was with him. That night, we all gathered at Bailey's. Dad was the centre of attention and clearly in his element, regaling the bar with tales of his life. Somehow, as the drinking gathered pace, the story was told of how we had arrived in Dublin with our pockets stuffed with English ten-pound notes. He laughed with us as we talked of getting the upper hand in a double bluff with some of London's most notorious gangsters. I think he was secretly proud of me.

Nick announced his return to London. I was furious and upset. We had established ourselves as a key attraction in the city and the money was pouring in. Why abandon that success?

As the troubles in Northern Ireland accelerated, security was at its height. Whatever the cause, I found myself banned from every pub. One quick glance at what was clearly my photograph in a rogue's gallery next to the till, and that was it. "Sorry, you're barred." I was humiliated and thirsty.

I knew it could only go from bad to worse. When the Special Branch gets you in their sights, there is nowhere to go. A return to busking in the city would be nigh impossible. Dublin was and is a great city. It is a city with values and strong traditions. I love that it celebrates its authors, playwrights, poets, musicians, talkers, and political activists. I felt at home there. Ireland was in my blood, and over the past few months I had established myself in the fabric of life in this fantastic city. Now I was being forced to leave. Mhairi agreed that my choices had run out in Dublin and urged me to return to Edinburgh—she would travel over in a few weeks.

The train to Belfast was surprisingly busy. There was real trouble there. The city was a tinderbox. My plan was to make for the ferry on arrival and get across the Irish Sea as swiftly as I could. As the train rolled through the countryside, I made my way to the buffet car. "A can of Smithwicks, please," I said. As I reached into my pocket, there was nothing there. It was empty. I searched every pocket. Nothing. I ran back to my seat. Nothing. I asked the guard. Nothing. I had been robbed. I was penniless as I arrived in Belfast, where British troops had just been deployed, tensions were at breaking point, and danger seemed to lurk on every street.

Jesus, I was in trouble!

I had to approach the situation calmly and logically. As we neared Belfast, I was struggling to think of solutions. The agencies that might be able to help were all closed for the night, and the streets would be empty. Remembering my Catholic roots, I had a sudden idea that seemed bulletproof. I would find a church and ask the priest for some support. Walking around Belfast was like walking on a tightrope. The tension was palpable, and as a stranger to its streets, I found it utterly terrifying. Who do you ask for directions to the nearest Catholic church in a city divided by religious sectarianism?

As people scurried homeward, the streets were emptying fast—only the troops seemed to be hanging around.

Finally, I spotted a church close to Donegal Road. Next to it was clearly the priest's house. The tension left my body as I composed myself for a quick explanation of my situation. I would be safe for the night and could arrange things the following morning. I rang the bell and waited a few moments before a craggy-faced priest opened the door. "Oh, Father, bless you. I am on my way home to Scotland, but I've been robbed. I am hungry and homeless tonight. If I can just phone my dad in Edinburgh...?" I begged. "Look, would you ever fuck off?" he barked, cutting my plea short and promptly shutting the door in my face.

Here was I, a former, albeit failed, altar boy, in trouble in a city overrun by troops and riven by tensions, bombings, and killings—being turned away by a priest. It was devastating.

'Where next? The police'.

I found a police station heavily defended by strong wooden gates. Again, I rang the bell. It took an age before a small, eye-level shutter was opened, and a disembodied voice asked me what I wanted. I told him my story as succinctly as I could, and he at least had a suggestion for me. "Go to the bus station, get into one of the buses, and stay there until the morning." The shutter was then slammed shut, and I was left once again to my own devices.

The bus station was easy to find, thanks to a policeman's directional advice. As suggested, there were empty buses there. I chose one that was as obscured from view as possible. I climbed to the top deck and lay across the back seat. I was exhausted and just about to enter that semi-conscious state when there was an almighty clatter on the stairs. I had barely registered the sound when an Alsatian's jaw gripped the seat of my trousers and tore some of the fabric away. There was a flash of torchlight, and my tormentor called me to heel. "Jesus, I was only trying to get a night's kip, not steal the fucking bus." "Sorry, pal, you'll have to find somewhere else." "It was the police that told me to come here." "What the fuck do those bastards know?" he said, guiding me off the bus. He was clearly a Catholic.

I was out in the street again.

I somehow survived the night, and the next day I was able to get help from the social security office to return to Edinburgh. I had been in my dad's new flat only fleetingly before. Now traumatised by my night in Belfast, exhausted by the journey, and with the seat of my pants torn off, it felt like the most wonderful place on earth.

Dad welcomed me with a meal of duck al'orange—the irony of his dish choice after my Belfast experience was not lost on me. "Mike," he said, "I hope you are going to settle here for a while. This is your home." There was a tear in his eye as he spoke. It was never said, but he knew that his infidelity had broken his family, and each of us had suffered in various ways. Guilt was written all over his face, but he didn't know how to express it. "It's okay, Dad; I understand."

We then moved on to the imminent arrival of Mhairi. He was thrilled by this news. I sensed the start of a new adventure. For now, at least, I have some space to breathe. What I was to discover over the coming months and years was that my father had become a highly accomplished cook, able to produce one delightful meal after another. If I hadn't returned to consuming copious quantities of amphetamines, I would have put on a few pounds.

CHAPTER 29

Tale of Two Cities

After those tumultuous few years, it was never going to be easy to settle into home life. I was older, had experienced life on the streets, skirted a life of crime, and held the attention of audiences in Dublin. I had been beaten, spat on, touched by the sharp blade of a knife, and treated at times like an animal. I had also been lauded and applauded. I felt stronger and more resilient. Yet somehow being at home brought back something of the frightened child in me.

The first few weeks in Edinburgh were quiet and uneventful, and when Mhairi arrived from Dublin, I took pride in Edinburgh and what it had to offer—it is a special city, especially when you view it through the eyes of someone seeing it for the first time. Mhairi loved Edinburgh and, because of its Celtic culture, adjusted easily to life in the city.

As far as finding a job, I landed a night shift at a biscuit factory. I was assigned to the shortbread belt, where my job was to place the steel moulds on the sweetened dough just before it entered the oven. The result at the end of production was what you see in a shortbread variety tin. It was really hot where I was stationed, and I felt under such pressure as the belt speeded up through the night. Most of my co-workers were ex-cons from Edinburgh Prison. The bad news for them was that after a night or two, I was able to perform my task with my eyes shut. It was tedious work, but I gave it my all, which was quickly noted by the bosses, and I was seen as a diligent employee.

This earned me a promotion to Jaffa Cake production and a new white overall featuring a graphic of the Jaffa Cake on my chest. I really looked the part now with my hairnet and nifty new overalls. My sudden elevation to the world of chocolate and marmalade drew derision from my former colleagues, who saw my move as a betrayal of shortbread solidarity. "Fucking snob!" they would shout as I appeared for work each night. Saturday morning was treat time, and I would return home with a brown paper bag stuffed with broken biscuits. With that level of corporate generosity, it's hard to see why industrial relations in this country sometimes descend into chaos.

My career in biscuits was to end after just six weeks into the job. Held overnight in a cell, my perfect attendance record was broken, and I never returned to the factory. It was all so unfair. Due to appearing in court as a witness to a break-in at 10 a.m., I returned home from my overnight shift, opted to stay awake, and sat in a chair. I just could not prevent myself from drifting off to sleep. I awoke to the awful realisation that I'd missed my court date. I called the court to explain. They told me to call the police, which I promptly did, only to be told that it was a court matter. Frustrated and exhausted, I gave up and went to bed for a well-deserved rest.

That evening, just as I was about to set off for work, the doorbell rang. My dad answered. Here were two policemen with a warrant for my arrest. As I was taken into police custody, my father was incandescent. "For fuck sake; he's on night shift and fell asleep. He's not a bloody criminal," he shouted. It was all in vain.

I was to share my cell that evening with a guy who was pissed and incontinent and a bunch of Ranger supporters arrested for fighting. I tried to stay awake, but my body was screaming for a rest. The irony of this all is that the guy whose case I was to appear in that morning walked free while I spent a night in a cell and received a fine for contempt of court. I had felt I was making progress, but this set me back. What kind of establishment would punish me for an honest mistake while allowing the offender to walk free? I had been told that my dream career option was as a refuse collector. I managed to find myself a job in a biscuit factory, and then effectively lost it because I had fallen asleep after twenty waking hours and a hard night's work.

I had been so disciplined about it all—resisting the temptation of a social life with friends and getting on that bus to work at the appointed time each evening. The pattern had been broken.

Yet again, I was experiencing the inhumanity of frontline services and their lack of empathy. I was feeling lower than I had for a while. I didn't sign on because I wanted to stay away from people who sat behind desks and neither listened nor cared.

I wanted to feel valued, as I had in Dublin.

As an alternative, I wanted the exhilaration that came with my drugs of choice, speed and acid, and planned a trip to London to stock up.

Mhairi was becoming a victim of my restlessness and self-pity. We were slowly drifting apart, and in truth, I wasn't being kind to her. I was hardly ever home, and she was left to her own devices for hours on end. When she met Brian Reid, I was delighted. His flat had become a venue for after-hours socialising. Brian was an outdoor type whose passions were fishing and climbing, and he clearly liked Mhairi. The last thing I wanted was for her to suffer, and when she announced that she was planning to move in with him, I was sad but relieved. Brian did me a huge favour.

She made the right move. I was beginning to drift back into the world of drugs, while she had ambitions to do something with her

145

life. Months later, she and Brian moved to Oban, took over a fishing boat, made good money, and then bought a local hotel.

Over the years, their business empire expanded, and I hear they did very well indeed. I was glad for her and pleased that her move to Scotland, which I had engineered, had been rewarded.

I hitchhiked to London and back to the places I knew best. On my very first day, minutes after my arrival in the city centre, I was attacked on the steps leading down to Piccadilly Underground Station. My attacker recognised me from Edinburgh and accused me of chasing his girlfriend. I had no recollection whatsoever, but this was no time to mount a defence. I was taken by surprise—punched, kicked, and ultimately pushed down the stairs. Knocking a few startled commuters off their feet, I landed with my neck twisted and covered in cuts and bruises. One day back, I was in Charing Cross Hospital getting repairs done. This was not as I had planned. My trip had a clear purpose—to stock up on pills and make a speedy return to Edinburgh. Dad had been saddened and fearful about my departure, but I had assured him that I would be back in a matter of days. I miscalculated badly.

The next day, I met my old friend Terry, still holding court in the shadows of Eros. Pleased to see me, he gave me a plentiful supply of Black Bombers and Dexedrine. One thing was certain: I would not go back on the streets. I had an address in Holland Park that had been given to me, and I tentatively headed there for some shelter. This was where Marcus, who had apparently forgiven me for sleeping with his girlfriend, now lived. The set-up in his flat was quite sophisticated. I heard music playing as I approached the door. There were cushions scattered around the floor and oriental-patterned fabrics draped over and around the furniture.

The girls who shared the flat were beautiful, and the scent of their perfume created a soft and richly sensual atmosphere. I found their air of femininity reassuring and their propensity for conversation stimulating. I would stoke myself with speed morning, noon, and night. There was always someone to talk to, and I felt alive in the world. Someone had bought the Beatles White album, and I would listen to each song's instrumentation and chord formations for hours on end. I didn't have a guitar, so all this was played in my imagination. I couldn't wait to start playing again. For days on end, I would sit rocking back and forth, listening to the music and playing it over and over in my head. When the girls were around, the conversation was sharp and stimulating. As the weeks passed, so did my consumption of speed.

"There's no food," someone shouted from the kitchen one night, and we have no money. I'd been there for a number of weeks now, and here was a chance to repay the hospitality. "Don't worry, I'll go out and find some," I promised. I can't remember who offered to accompany me, but it was 5:00 a.m. when we set out on our hunt. We scoured the restaurants looking for deliveries of bread, but there was nothing. Just then, a Grimsby truck pulled up alongside one of the restaurants. We watched with great excitement as one crate after another was piled up inside the doorway. When the truck moved off, we made our catch. We took two of the crates of freshly caught fish and made our way back to the flat to be greeted with howls of enthusiasm. Suddenly everyone was awake, and the kitchen was a hive of bustling activity. Fried, boiled, and baked fish dishes were being produced and plated one after the other.

I had scaled the wall and returned triumphant.

By that evening, we were sated and stoned amid the overpowering smell of fish. When the police arrived, the evidence for the prosecution was in such abundance that I could only take it up immediately. The police found the situation funny, but took us to the cells nonetheless. "We have a cell, and we want to 'fillet'," laughed one uniformed joker—a Glaswegian. One night and a day later, I was released with a stern warning. "Call it an early Christmas present," said the sergeant. "Oh fuck. It's Christmas!" I had no idea. I was so drugged up that it had passed me by. It was Christmas Eve, and I had no way of getting home. I'd promised my dad that I would share a Christmas dinner with him for the first time in years, and I had told my mum that I would pay a visit to see her and Tony on Boxing Day.

CHAPTER 30

Penniless & Weightless

I returned to the flat. I had lost so many pounds that I looked like a pale imitation of my former self. The flat was virtually empty over Christmas; I felt alone and depressed. Each high I got with the speed was inevitably followed by a low—the feeling of emptiness was getting worse with each comedown. Speed is no weapon against depression—it simply degenerates the condition.

On Christmas Day, I decided to walk the streets. I saw families laden with bright, colourful gifts, Christmas lights sparkling in windows, party sounds emanating from pubs and homes, laughter and joy, kissing and hugging, and the aroma of roasting turkey—it was torture. I was very cold and very hungry. Only one clear thought began to crystallise.

I wanted to end it. I'd had enough.

I felt worthless and depressed. The river was within reach. As I wandered into Notting Hill Gate, I thought I was going to pass out. Holding onto railings, my legs began to give up on me.

Just then, something miraculous happened. I heard a woman's voice. "Cat, is that you?" I turned and saw nothing. I was surely imagining things. "It is Cat!" screamed an excited voice. It came from the doorway of a basement flat. "Jenny!" I couldn't believe it. Here was a girl I had befriended at Kensington Antique Market more than a year earlier. She looked and smelled glorious as she embraced me. "I thought I would never see you again; you look terrible! Come in for something to eat and meet my mum and sister."

Out of the darkness had come a broad beam of light. I had been saved from the edge. Jenny was lovely, and so was her family. They even gave me gifts of aftershave and chocolate. The flat had Jenny's fingerprints everywhere—she was an artist, and her design details were exquisite. I ate slowly, taking a small piece at a time. My stomach had shrunk, and my capacity for food had greatly reduced.

I camped out on the couch that night. My sleep was fitful, and I kept waking to thoughts of my family back in Scotland: Dad and Brian in Edinburgh, Mum and Tony in Glenrothes. The tears came fast and furious. What had I become—consumed by drugs, painfully thin, and without any hope? I had let my family down, and I had let myself down. I had so much promise, and there was so much I wanted to do, but who would employ me with my record? I had put my family through enough worry as it was, and I was desperate to redeem myself, but how and where? It was difficult to see a way forward.

Jenny floated into the living room, took my hand, and kissed me. Wearing a white Victorian nightgown, she really did look like an angel. Her skin was so soft and fragrant that I felt transported into a fantasy. "Cat," she whispered, "what has happened?" I gave her an edited version of the past year—the highs and lows of Dublin, the return to Edinburgh, and the descent back into drugs. "I'll get you a ticket back to Edinburgh," she promised, "but stay with me for a few days."

My time in Notting Hill was restorative. Jenny is one of the nicest people I have ever met. I never spoke to her again, and every attempt to trace her since has been unsuccessful. That's because I delayed getting in touch. She took me in when I was at my lowest point, and her intervention was a delightful bolt from the blue. Had she not seen me on that Christmas Day, I might have ended up at the bottom of the Thames—I really had been that low.

The bus out of Victoria two weeks later was packed. I sat with my head resting on the cool window, deep in thought. Why did every public agency I dealt with treat me like an idiot—toxic and unwashed? Would I ever gain enough credibility to get some leverage with them? Looking for a job was going to be tricky. I'd had six jobs and been sacked from half of them. I searched my pocket for black bombers and consumed the remaining three. I couldn't sleep in any case, and I wanted to be well prepared for my arrival in Edinburgh.

As we entered the city through the old Dalkeith Road, lights were being switched on in tenement windows. Edinburgh was slowly awakening from its slumber, and the sky was streaked with burning orange. The greyness of the buildings was strangely reassuring. There is a solidity about Edinburgh. This is a city that has given the world so much in world-changing ideas and inventions, yet keeps its achievements buttoned up. It exudes a quiet and understated confidence that few cities can match. I was glad to be home, and this time I wanted to make it back for good.

Dad was pleased to see me but shocked by my appearance. The weighing scales told a story. I was now seven and a half stones— lighter than I had been at fourteen years old. My hair was long and dishevelled; my skin was pale; and my eyes were red and baggy. Dad made me a breakfast of eggs and bacon, which I feasted on before sleeping late into the day.

It was time to reconnect with people I knew in the city and get a place to stay. My feet had barely touched the Scottish earth, but I didn't want to burden Dad and subject him to the horrors of my chemical habits. So, two days later, I moved into a small flat just off

Morrison Street. My flatmates were new to me. Tam and Gavin, both from Fife, were permanently stoned and always willing to share their spoils with me.

I was now using acid on top of the speed and was on a permanent high. I saw this as a temporary situation that I would deal with after I'd settled back into life in Edinburgh. Meanwhile, I was making lots of friends, and each night the flat would fill up with strangers—by morning, we were lifelong buddies. I loved talking, and the conversations were unceasing—but I was now entering a new phase. I would forget where I was and lose any sense of time. I thought my nadir came when I was picked up by the police talking to an imaginary audience in Princes Street, but I was wrong—worse was still to follow. The police phoned my father, and I was only released on the promise that I would be seen by a specialist doctor. I realised the next day that this was a euphemism for a psychiatrist.

The next day, I saw the 'specialist' doctor.

Under examination, the physical and mental cracks began to appear. I was a mess. I was referred immediately to the Royal Edinburgh Hospital—a psychiatric hospital. Memories of my stay there are hazy, but I made a mistake that nearly cost me my life and shook my dad to the core. A few days into my stay, I was allowed to walk on the hospital grounds. I was on a prescribed dose of Largactil, and when I took a couple of pills from a friend during my walkabout, the result was catastrophic. The drugs reacted badly. My next memory was of lying in bed with my dad in tears as a doctor explained to him that I had been only moments away from a brain haemorrhage. A few days later, I discharged myself and pledged that I would never allow drugs to rule my life again.

I was true to my word.

I agreed to move back in with Dad, took a trip to see Mum and Tony, and set about job seeking. I was angry with myself for being so easily knocked sideways by events and knew that if I was to begin to climb back and fulfill anything like my potential, I was going to have to learn to take things on the chin. I was offered a job as an orderly at Queensberry House, which is hideously described as a terminal hospital. Many of the older people had dementia; all carried horrible bedsores, and too many had been abandoned and seemingly forgotten by their relatives. I felt enormous responsibility for their welfare and did all I could to bring some laughter and variety to their day. The routine was created by and for the staff. I was appalled by some of what I saw. You quickly learn that keeping patients in their beds minimises hassle and speeds up turnover.

They were manhandled with little or no warning. It was inhuman.

I remember one man arriving to be admitted. He was immaculately turned out—his shoes were highly polished, his blazer and trousers neatly pressed, and his tie was held with a glistening gold tie pin. He sat alone, and you could see by his facial expressions and body language the slow realisation that was where it was to end. I don't know what story his relatives had spun him, but he knew. He took a look around to see that he was the only person dressed up, and in any way mobile. A few days later, he was bedridden like all the other poor souls who had been dumped there.

I learned the value of listening to older people's life stories. Here I was faced with people who had lived through two great wars, yet our response to their contribution was to deposit them in a terminal hospital and leave them to die. Each day I was hearing remarkable tales of lives lived and lost, of triumphs and disappointments, of poverty, adversity, achievement, and creativity. Yet I watched other colleagues roll their eyes and say to them, "Not another war story," and cut them short.

It's true that each day their bedclothes were replaced, their bedsores were dressed, and they could eat three meals a day—but that was it. I would use humour and laughter as much as I could, and that was great therapy for them. When they laughed, their smiles changed, and their eyes began to light up. Dignity is the least people deserve, and yet we are parsimonious and selective about what we afford people.

When my mother died in recent years, bringing a smile to her face became my mission each time I saw her. I know she loved that.

I had learned from my own experiences on the street and then trying to deal with the plethora of agencies, from the NHS to the banks, the damage done by those who use policies and procedures to thwart progress. I had encountered people who could never step beyond the job description and retreated behind the rulebook. I would imagine an alternative society where the whole notion of privilege was abandoned and each individual had the same right to respect and dignity.

"Och, you're an idealist," they would say. But in the pubs around Edinburgh, I was meeting people who understood what I was saying and felt the same way.

CHAPTER 31

Striped Pyjamas

It was during a drinking session at Paddy's Bar in Rose Street that Cathy entered my life. She was staring into the tropical fish tank when I observed that some of the fish were clearly ready for bed because they were wearing their striped pyjamas. Hardly a line out of the Oscar Wilde book of gems, but her laugh started an affair that endured on and off for years, then moved in later years to a strong friendship. She is now a well-respected academic at Auckland University. Cathy was gorgeous with her long, golden wavy hair, greenish eyes, and lovely, smiling freckled face. Our mutual attraction was immediate. Conversation flowed easily with Cathy. I was so happy to have met her. I danced all the way back to my flat that night, arranging to meet Cathy the following day.

I introduced her to Dad a few days later, and much to my delight, they hit it off. Work at Queensberry House was giving me a regular income, and joyously, Dad agreed to stand as guarantor on a higher purchase agreement when I saw and fell in love with a guitar I'd seen in a shop window. It was a Levin 12-string, made in Sweden with cedar wood.

When Cathy heard me play and sing, she was enthralled—especially by my rendition of Donovan's "Catch the Wind". "You have real talent. We have to do something about getting you noticed." She and her older sister, Margaret, joined forces, made tapes, and approached record companies. I would spend days and nights at their home in Clermiston while they fed me home-made chips and endless cups of tea. Their mum was fantastic and didn't mind the intrusion. I was being gently fattened, and with their love and care, I began to make real progress. A few asthma attacks interrupted that progress, but I was coming alive at last. I played and played wherever there was an opportunity—on the streets, at impromptu concerts, and in pubs. One evening I walked into every restaurant and café I could find in the city centre and sang a song as the waiting staff looked on in utter astonishment.

My brother Brian was now back in Edinburgh, and we were introduced to Dan, a director at the Traverse Theatre, and Martin, a wealthy architect, who wanted to stage a show at that year's Fringe Festival. Martin had taken over the old Edinburgh Rock factory on Victoria Street's upper terrace. He had kitted it out as a theatre and was keen to put something on. We gathered a few friends and somehow put something together—it was an awful mix of comedy sketches and music, but we got a wonderful experience putting a show together. Without Dan's expert direction, Lord knows what chaos would have ensued. The show went ahead, and we attracted packed audiences for an entire week.

My relationship with Cathy was going well, although I also had a relationship with her sister Maggie—it was all in the open, and there was nothing sordid about it. As we approached the summer of 1971, I was getting itchy feet again and wanted to return to London. I wanted London to see a different side of me and for me to experience the city with money in my pocket. With my twenty-first birthday fast approaching, my dad was keen to mark the occasion with a party at his flat.

The day of my birthday started well. In the midst of a collection of birthday cards sat a brown envelope, which I was about to discard when Dad interjected. "Why not open that first and get it out of the way?" It was a tax rebate. I was astonished. A birthday surprise from the Inland Revenue? Life was surely on the up. In the lead up to the party, I had become more and more choked by a cold, so as the guests arrived later that evening, I sat with my head under a towel, inhaling from a bowl of hot water and Friar's Balsam.

Among my guests were Ian and Nigel. "We're off to London tomorrow, and we've found a civil service hostel to live in. All we have to do is pretend that we have jobs in the Civil Service, and we're in." "Where is it?" I asked. Ian rummaged in his pocket and pulled out a piece of paper. "It's in Cadogan Square, just off Sloane Square and Kings Road."

"Fuck! You're joking, aren't you?"

That night, plans were plotted. I was going back to London. This time, I would not fall victim to its streets. I was ready. Cathy was also planning to stretch her wings and said she would also make an appearance in London sometime soon.

CHAPTER 32

A New Work Ethic

When the bus arrived at Victoria Station, I had a packed bag and a destination. I felt good about myself and couldn't wait to touch base with the others at the hostel. I had been to Cadogan Square once before with Jenny on a 'how the other half lives' tour, and now I was about to take up residence in this centre of opulence. Cadogan Square is the third-most expensive street in Britain. Jenny had explained to me two years before that the architecture was Flemish in influence and that this would be her dream location to live. If only she could see me now.

When I arrived, I was not surprised to see that our accommodation was at the lower end of the market. It was situated in a very short mews off the square, but for me in London, this was luxury living. I was to share a room with Ian, who'd left Edinburgh a week before, and Phil, a librarian from Shropshire with a ginger comb-over hairstyle and a beard. Phil was quiet and tentative at first. But I quickly discerned that he was a lovely, gentle, and caring person.

I got a job within a day at Moss Bros. in Covent Garden, packing and dispatching hire suits. We were located in a large below-ground room with no natural light. Sol, my supervisor, took his role very seriously, and I would get away with nothing less than perfectly folded clothes and well-wrapped boxes. I liked Sol's meticulous attention to detail, and despite incurring his wrath on a number of occasions, I learned to do things well—to fold a suit and shirts using tissue paper in the right measure and in the right places, tie parcel knots with string and sometimes ribbon. I valued each little piece of the learning jigsaw by watching, listening, and practising. I didn't like being so detached from the rest of the store, especially where all the girls worked, but I was also free from distraction. Apart from Sol, an East End Jew, most of my colleagues were Mauritian. I learned from them about their country, their food, and their culture.

Approach any job as a valuable learning experience; give it everything you've got; follow those that do rather than those that don't; and you go home with an extra spring in your step. I made up my mind that I would be the most punctual, enthusiastic, and hardworking employee—wherever I worked. I did everything right at Moss Bros. and knew that if called on, they would give a decent reference. I loved getting up in the morning with a sense of purpose, jumping on a tube train, and joining the throngs of commuters.

Ian had secured a job at a wine cellar in Victoria, so when he told me of a job vacancy, I jumped at the chance. Within a week, I was installed as a wine corker. The company imported wine from France, bottled, labelled, and distributed it in the UK. Its customers included Julian Bream, who would regularly show up for tastings, and the House of Commons. My job was to keep the corks wet, place them for corking, and pull the lever down to meet the mouth of the bottle. Miss the bottle or allow the cork to get too dry, and the bottle would explode.

I liked the job and the people who worked there. My favourite had to be Glaswegian Tam. Not out of some misplaced national solidarity but because here was a guy assigned to a small, airless room away from everyone whose life consisted of manually filling bottles with grenadine. He'd apparently started on wine but would consume it in such large quantities that he would rarely be sober. Now, he was entrusted only with fruit syrups. He only ever appeared at break times but was a laugh a minute. You could see why he was retained rather than sacked after his drinking escapades. In fact, this was a brilliant piece of man management— Tam was liked by everyone and was one of these people who brought people together and was ever able to diffuse tensions.

I was at the sharp end, learning about French wines and taking a couple of half bottles back to my room each night. I explained to the woman who ran the hostel about my undercover role at Customs and Excise, telling her that the bottles that clanked each night when I returned from work were confiscated contraband. Her wry smile told me that she believed none of it but would stay mum about it.

Over the next couple of months, I bottled Rose d'Anjou and Beaujolais. We also imported bottled wine, and the cellars were stocked with Gewürztraminer, Chateauneuf du Pape, Chablis, and Muscadet. My wine collection was growing by the day. When it came to Christmas and a return home to Edinburgh, I packed a suitcase with one shirt, one pair of trousers, and 26 half bottles of wine.

My trip home was a triumphant one. I arrived with money, newfound status, and a mini-wine cellar. Dad cooked up a goose on Christmas Day, which we washed down with what I was now able to agree was a delightful French wine—his selection. I went to Glenrothes to see Mum and Tony the day after Boxing Day, and that was a success. Mum now worked as a receptionist in a doctor's surgery and seemed to be holding her life together. Tony, at eleven, was a truly beautiful boy and a delight to be with. I felt like I was acquainting myself with him all over again. It had been so long since I had allowed myself to get close to my family. I almost cried when Mum served up a homemade pizza for dinner—cheese, tomatoes, anchovies, prawns, and olives. I was transported back to all those exotic flavours of my childhood.

Mum talked of her work and I of mine. When I was about to leave, she hugged me tightly and told me she was proud of me. I waited until I was on the train before I allowed myself to cry. I felt that I had restored some of the damage. My years off the radar must have caused them so much anxiety. I felt desperately sad about what I had put them through. I had been needlessly neglectful of Mum before I left home—it was as if I blamed her for Dad's transgression, and yet, all she had done was tell me about it. I loved her so much and felt saddened by what must have been a massive change in her lifestyle. I couldn't muster any anger against my father, and to this day I cannot understand why. His actions had humiliated all of us, and the consequences had been awful for all of us. Yet the relationship that had ripped the family apart had lasted no longer than four years.

During my stay, everyone commented on how much better I looked. I was ready to return to London; my confidence and spirits were high. The wine business was good, and the company's owner, Mr. Reynier, had clearly been fed some good reports about my performance. A full attendance record, no flare-ups, and a willingness to learn and take on more responsibility. I'd even volunteered to work overnight as Reynier's sought the use of a helicopter to try and win the race to get the first bottle of Beaujolais Nouveau to these shores. We missed the prize, but only by a whisker. It was also proving to be my most hazardous job. During my time there, I accumulated five stitches and a skin graft on my right hand.

In any case, I was invited into a maroon Jaguar and taken on a PR visit to some of our most favoured customers. If it hadn't been for a chance to triple my earnings at a stroke, I may have done very, very well in the wine industry.

My motivation to raise my earnings was love. Since my return from home, I had been dating an auburn-haired Canadian girl named Lisa. She would only be in London for another six weeks, and I had fallen head over heels for her. She was tactile, easy to talk to, and had a great laugh. Whatever we did together was enjoyable. A simple walk to the tube station would become an adventure. What

I wanted more than anything was to be able to treat Lisa to dinner before she returned to Canada. I'd seen a restaurant off the Kings Road that I wanted to take her to, but it was well beyond my price range.

"Why don't you join the building trade?" suggested a Geordie friend that evening in the pub. "The pay's much better. If you work on the lump sum," it's all cash with no tax or national insurance to pay". I was taking home around £16 a week, and he was suggesting that I could pick up £60 to £80 each week—cash in hand. It was a no-brainer. Next lunchtime, I called a builder that had been recommended. He invited me to report to work the following Monday. The address was a building site in the east end.

They were really disappointed to hear of my departure from Reynier's, and in truth, so was I. It had been a great place to work; I had learned so much, and there were real prospects of progression for me. But for the last time in my life, I made the pursuit of money my priority. Short-term greed never leads to long-term gain. That is a value I learned then and have retained all of my life.

On Monday morning, after a seemingly endless tube journey, I arrived in Stratford, ready for my new working life. I was working for a subcontractor who provided bricklaying and plastering services. My first job was as a plasterer's labourer. On my first day, I carried bags of plaster up and down one level of scaffolding, then mixed the plaster, ensuring that two plasterers always had a plentiful supply to apply their magic to the walls. By the end of the day, I was both tired and exhilarated. I slept deeply that night and was up, ready, and enthused early the next day. I loved the physical side of the job and worked like a Trojan for the two weeks we were on site.

Our wages were delivered in cash through the window of a Jaguar. In just two weeks, I had made £120. More importantly, my health was benefiting from the relentless physical exercise I was getting. We completed a couple of domestic building jobs over the following few weeks, one in a mews flat in Chelsea and the other at a mansion in Kingston-on-Thames. The latter belonged to a dairy millionaire who wanted to build at the foot of his enormous garden. He had a little girl of around nine who would watch us for hours on end. Her face would light up if one of us waved or smiled at her. Each day, she would draw closer and closer to where we were working. I saw nothing but sadness etched in her young face. She was always alone, and anytime she attempted a conversation with us, her mother would come racing out of the house, grab her arm, and drag her inside. This wee lassie will inherit her parents' millions, but as a child, she was lonely and sad. What she needed was play, fun, laughter, and stimulus in her life—not the promise of wealth in her adulthood.

At that moment, I had a fleeting thought that one day I would like to work with small children. I recalled the enormous impact those cheery window cleaners had on my childhood and how they broke the tedium with a smile, a joke, and a ruffle of my hair. They belonged to a world of camaraderie, whistled as they worked, and were always on the move. I saw myself through the eyes of this child. I had become one of those window cleaners, capable of bringing some joy into her life. When we were packing to leave the site after a few weeks, I saw her at a window with tears rolling down her cheeks. I asked her mum if I could say goodbye to her, and she refused.

Lisa was now close to leaving the UK, and I was dreading her departure. Our relationship was flourishing, and she had filled a space in my life I didn't even know existed. I was complete when I was with Lisa, and heaven knows what might have happened if we had been able to stay together. Meanwhile, I had pledged to take her for a slap-up meal in Chelsea, and now, with money in my pocket and a rudimentary knowledge of wine, I was ready to fulfil that promise. That night we ate like royalty and drank like lords, and two days later, as we said our goodbyes, our digestive systems were still working on overdrive.

CHAPTER 33

Cat Stevens

A few weeks later, I received a letter from Lisa, urging me to listen to Cat Stevens' Tea for the Tillerman album. I knew which song she wanted me to hear, "Sad Lisa". I never made contact with her again. In today's digitally connected world, it is difficult to recall just how challenging it was to maintain a relationship across the Atlantic Ocean.

"Your body is changing shape," said the guys at the hostel. I looked in the mirror, and it was true. My upper body now resembled that of a middleweight boxer. I was stronger, bulkier, and healthier in almost every way, and I was tanned by the early spring sun. The asthma attacks were becoming less frequent, and I was full of energy and ideas. When I joined the others in the Markham Bar on Kings Road each evening, I saw in them a different kind of energy— loosened ties, shoulders dropped, and stifled yawns. The Civil Service provided a contrasting challenge to that of a building site. I was happy to be working on something that led to a tangible product. Physical work tires the body, but it refreshes and reinvigorates the mind. I was full of humour and chatter in the evenings and was gaining a reputation as a raconteur. I would talk to anyone anywhere without the aid of chemicals.

The Markham pub was my favourite venue, and I had an expanding group of friends. They came from all walks of life, from Alan Hudson, who played in the midfield for Chelsea, to Gordon, a former Mayor of Anglesey, who was portly, posh, and full of fun. Conversation is everything to me now, and the chance to talk and share stories, thoughts, and ideologies was utterly compelling. I met a friend recently who had shared some of those evenings on Kings Road back in 1971. When he heard that I was doing motivational speaking, he said, "I always knew you would use God's gift one day." I was astonished. He also mentioned that I had always been a great storyteller and could command an audience.

Kings Road was at the epicentre of British fashion at the time, and there were some miraculously beautiful people about. Models, poseurs, and fashionistas would wander among us. There was one couple that especially stood out for me. They were both unfeasibly beautiful—he with his perfectly permed hair, trimmed beard, and perfect blue eyes; she with a femininity and poise I had rarely seen before. There was nothing conventional in her beauty, and I couldn't keep my eyes off her. They would also stand apart from the crowd at the bar, and I saw her glimpse over a couple of times.

If only...

One evening, she arrived without her beau and a group of female friends. She looked over and smiled. A few seconds later, her friends glanced in my direction—this was my chance to introduce myself. I was thrilled to find that they were all Geordies and to find myself warmly welcomed. I couldn't keep my eyes off Linda, but it was her friend with the same name that latched onto me for the night. The other Linda was petite, with long dark hair and wild green eyes. Back in their flat later that evening, I slept with Linda, and as great as it was, I was still possessed by her namesake. Months later, my roommate moved back to Newcastle, promising to catch up with me whenever she could.

I cannot remember the context, but I spent a night at the girls' flat soon after. It was a troubled time for me. I was feeling a bit low and had drunk more than usual. I was on the couch that night, restless and unable to sleep. Linda wandered through and positioned herself beside me. We talked and we talked. I had dreamt of being this close to her, yet I was paralysed. Eventually, she clearly took my lack of affection as a rejection and returned to her room. Never, ever again, would I let an opportunity like that slip away. I saw then how my self-belief deserted me when something I really, really wanted was within my grasp.

How many people suffer from the same sense that they are not good enough when these opportunities arise? We sabotage our own chances again and again. This didn't sink in for years to come, and when I saw how I would shrink from what I desired most, I was horrified. How many life-changing chances had I failed to grasp? I then taught myself to recognise and go for opportunities without fear or hesitation. It may have come later in life, but it opened up a whole new world for me.

In London, I was slowly building my confidence. That confidence came from doing things well at work and learning something new each and every day. I was assigned to a building project in Covent Garden, which was by far the biggest and most complex I had experienced. This was the major conversion of a four-story building in the heart of London. "Do you think you can carry hods for the bricklayers?" I was asked. "Of course," I answered with unswerving confidence. That day, I carried piles of bricks on my right shoulder up and down tiers of scaffolding. It was more physically demanding than anything I had ever done, but I was in my element. I was getting supremely fit and picking up so much knowledge about the building trade. It was like a mind-body gym—a chance to stretch myself to my physical limits, enjoy the camaraderie of men, and learn new tricks.

My building career was punctuated by one moment of abject horror. On the top floor, I was asked to lower a wheelbarrow to the ground using the hook and trolley that were attached to the outside of the building. My grasp slipped, and the wheelbarrow plummeted four stories to the ground. Feeling sure I had killed somebody I froze to the spot. I couldn't bear to look below. "Who in fuck's name threw a wheelbarrow out the window?" shouted the foreman. "It was me," I confessed.

"Lucky, you never hurt anyone!"

My heart eventually settled into a steady beat, but there was a moment when time seemed to stand still. Surveying the scene below, I realised the carnage I could have caused. Thankfully, the incident was instantly forgotten, and I was able to get back to mixing cement and carrying piles of bricks without a blemish on my record. My jeans were now encrusted with splashes of dried plaster and cement, and my shirt was torn and stained, but I walked with pride and stood with my head held high in the tube.

Young men like nothing better than physical work and seeing the product of their labour.

Why academic study is still elevated so far above vocational skills defeats me to this day. This country was built by the labour of generation after generation. Our economy has never been so precarious as it is with financial services as a primary revenue source. Any society that draws its wealth from making money from money has lost its productive soul and any sense of value.

When I think back to the immense pride I took in making things, I see buildings with a new lease on life and new ones rising from the ground, glistening and confident. Being part of it is joyful. I can only imagine what it felt like on the Clyde when great ships were launched, in the car factories where shiny new lean machines emerged onto our highways, and when, after risking life and limb to extract it, coal powered the nation.

Too much education from the neck up leaves us disembodied, inflexible, and fragile in this rapidly changing world. My head teacher years earlier disparaged industry as a destination for lesser intellectuals—yet some of the smartest, most creative, and most inventive people I have met scored low at school.

They learned by experiencing and doing.

The Forth Railway Bridge stands as a monument not just to the engineers that designed and tested it but to the thousands of men who, in all weathers and high above the inhospitable waters of the Firth of Forth, dug great granite pillars deep into the river bed and somehow used 25,000 tonnes of iron and rivets to create a structure still celebrated across the world as one of the great engineering accomplishments. Ninety-eight men lost their lives before it was opened in 1890.

CHAPTER 34

Part of a Bigger Picture

I learned a great lesson in leadership when I arrived at my next work destination, a building site on Earls Court Road. This was the build-from-scratch project starting on what was literally the ground floor. The one I mentioned earlier in the book.

On arrival, I was greeted by the Welsh site foreman sporting a tattered hat, a broken nose, and shovel-like hands that had grasped mine in a firm handshake. Wrapping an arm around my shoulder, he guided me a few steps. "Come with me; I have something I want to show you before you start." He led me to a temporary shack and showed me some drawings and a model of the proposed building. "This is the palace you are going to create," he said. "Picture it and remind yourself each day that everything you do is making this dream, a vision that someone had, come true."

From that moment on, I felt part of a bigger picture. Not a bit-part player. I was a vital cog in the wheel. I wanted to sweat buckets for this man. On all other sites, instructions had been barked at me: "Do this here and by this time." This man made me feel ten feet tall on that first day and each day that followed. He would regularly stop by with words of encouragement and advice. If I could do something better, he would thank me for what I'd done and then show me how to do it even faster and more effectively. He asked for favours rather than barked orders, and I was always keen to exceed expectations. He had a vision, which he shared. He equipped me with the tools and confidence to deliver on my part and kept me involved and motivated every step of the way. I was part of a team of bricklayers, plasterers, joiners, electricians, crane operators, labourers, pile-drivers, and glaziers from Ireland, the West Indies, Scotland, and all corners of England. We all knew each other's roles and supported each other. We were ready to step out of our prescribed role to help anyone who was falling behind. I was always early to start and late to leave. That was the power of one man's leadership. I learned so much from him.

Having seen London from the belly up, I was now experiencing a whole different perspective of the city, and as someone playing an albeit small part in building its fresh landscape, I felt I had a stake in it.

The hostel had brought together a great group of guys—Bob, Colin, Fred, and Phil, to name a few. We would drink during the evenings in the Markham Bar, and eat cheaply and plentifully at the Chelsea Kitchen. I loved having money in my pocket, eating out, dating girls, going to football matches at Chelsea or West Ham, and on weekends, finishing off the evenings at Café Des Artistes in Fulham. I met lots of women and dated a few. If they didn't have a flat, "come back to my hostel and meet my roommates" never ignited a spark. Phil's sister Anne, whom we would meet regularly for a drink, had a suggestion. "I saw a really nice flat in Shepherds Bush, but I need another two people to share the rent with me."

We moved in a couple of weeks later. It was an upper flat with its own side entry, a large, sunny living room, and two bedrooms. With my newfound skills in the building trade, I was happy to apply a few deft touches to the décor, and in a few days, we had created a fantastic space with a direct outlook onto busy, bustling Goldhawk Road.

I said my goodbyes to leafy Cadogan Square—to its air of affluent privilege and to a sexy secret. To explain, my room looked out on the narrow mews and directly into the large picture window opposite. I was delighted to discover soon after I moved in that the flat was home to a famous and beautiful film and television actress. If that wasn't enough to set any young man's pulse racing, she had a penchant for stripping slowly and erotically each night within full view of my window. This was an unspoken, but mutual arrangement; she knew and we knew. It was great while it lasted, but now glamour has been replaced by non-stop traffic.

I bought myself a second-hand bicycle and, from then on, cycled to work in Earls Court. It didn't seem that long ago that the streets, alleyways, and toilets of central London had been my home. Now I had the keys to a flat, a job, and my own means of transport. It was a liberation. I had a place where I could invite people to stay, cook my own meals, and play music into the early hours.

My brother Brian and his friend Paul came to stay, and Cathy came to visit. I hadn't touched a drug for ages and I had gained in strength, physique, and confidence. I still drank at the Markham pub, and my circle of friends was expanding. I was aware of a lot of gay interest in me and was as flattered by male attention as I was by that of the opposite sex. In fact, I enjoyed gay company a lot because they looked at life from a different perspective, always seemed up for a laugh, and were always kind to me. I did experiment a few times, but while I enjoyed some wildly exciting encounters with men, I knew I would always prefer women. I had some amazing offers from very wealthy and influential men who I could so easily have exploited, but I was never tempted. I knew how unrequited love felt.

When my dad announced a visit to London, I was excited. I couldn't wait to show him how I was prospering in my new life. We met for breakfast on Oxford Street, and I could see he was blown away by the change he saw in me. He kept looking at me and smiling to himself as I tucked into an enormous plateful of poached eggs and bacon. When I returned from a trip to the toilet, I caught sight of him wiping a tear from his eye. I remembered that expression of horror when I lay in that hospital bed, having narrowly escaped death.

The journey I had travelled in the past few years had been remarkable, and I began to see a future pan out. Later, dad joined my friends at the Markham Bar and managed to charm each and every one of them. I was so proud of him that night.

I knew that this trip was leading up to something. Before he left London, Dad had shown me a newspaper clipping. It was an advertisement for Newbattle Abbey College, near Edinburgh, for a year's residential study. This was a college funded by the Scottish Education Department and supported by trade unions to give a second chance to people who had failed to make the grade at school.

I read it over and over again.

I couldn't believe what was offered.

The only entry requirements were life experience, an enthusiasm to learn, and a failed experience in school education. It would be grant-aided, and despite having not even reached O-level standards at school, I would get a chance to sit Highers and A-levels. It was a lot to weigh up. I was settled in London. I had a flat, friends, connections, and money. But here was a chance to prove that I was capable of studying. I told Dad that I would sleep on it and let him know what I had decided.

When I called him two days later, he was full of anticipation. "I'll apply," I said. He was absolutely over the moon. He then told me that he'd taken the precaution of having a word with the college principal, who, having heard some of my story, was keen to meet me in London within the month.

I turned up for my interview suited, tied, and nervous. How was I to impress a man of letters? Charles Rigg was serious, deliberate, and measured—but encouraging throughout the discussion. He explained how Newbattle Abbey College had been founded in 1937 when the 11th Marquis of Lothian gifted his 16th-century home to the Scottish nation. The Marquis wanted to give adults a second chance to access education.

Mr. Rigg also told me that the building was originally a 12th-century Cistercian monastery, set in extensive woodlands with its own Italian garden on the banks of the River Esk.

I was sold, but had I impressed him? When we finished our discussion, he shook my hand, and as I made to leave, he uttered words that I'll never forget. "I look forward to welcoming you to Newbattle Abbey College in September." I ran to the nearest telephone box and called Dad.

"I've been accepted!" I screamed.

I was looking and feeling much healthier.

CHAPTER 35

College Days

The more I experience life, the more magical, evocative, and deeply meaningful poetry becomes. Life provides reference points along the way and gives meaning to thoughts, emotions, actions, pictures, and objects. At school, poetry was a chore, a box to tick—we had no real insight or appreciation. Now here I was, seven years later, discussing and enjoying the richness and subtleties of W.B. Yeats.

"Had I the heavens' embroidered cloths,
Enwrought with golden and silver light,
The blue and the dim and the dark cloths
Of night and light and the half-light,
I would spread the cloths under your feet.
But I, being poor, have only my dreams;
I have spread my dreams under your feet;
Tread softly because you tread on my dreams."

Words had always fascinated me, but I was seeing a new beauty in them—a world of vivid pictures that reached into our minds and our spirits. I was used to being summed up in simple pejoratives—waster, rough sleeper, stupid, inattentive, distracted, industrial only, etc. Yet here was a language that stretched far beyond lazy descriptions. I was gripped.

I had chosen to study English literature and government and politics at college. Learning in this way was a new discipline for me that I was slowly adapting to. Concepts and philosophies began to resonate with me in a way that would have been impossible at school, and I was sharing the experience with people like me who had in some way failed at school. Postmen, factory workers, refuse collectors, and waitresses I thought of those people I had shared the streets with in London and how they would benefit as much as I would from a second chance.

But for them, society had the lowest of low expectations. The die had been cast for many at birth. Some had been thrown off course by familial breakups, fallouts at home, and episodes of abuse. Many were so traumatising that they had been reduced to a horrible and tortured existence, waiting to be kicked again.

I knew how easy it is to feel alienated and devalued, to enter the slough of despond—that slow, relentless slide into a sense of utter worthlessness. It is a state of mind that puts us in the grip of paralysis and allows politicians and the intellectually moribund to dismiss us with easy descriptions. Yet here I was to meet the brightest, most creative, and intellectually astute people I could ever hope to meet, and I would learn immeasurably from them.

Sweeping up the driveway on that first day at Newbattle, I was struck by the immensity of its scale and grandeur—it was right out of a PG Wodehouse novel. I imagined myself as a weekend guest arriving at a country mansion. On both sides were sweeping lawns and mature trees, fringed by an expanse of woodland. It was a warm and sunny September afternoon, and cars and taxis were arriving in droves—suitcases, guitars, and even a teddy bear were emerging from vehicles in the grip of excited mature students-to-be.

In the imposing reception area, there were people of all hues and ages milling about. The place was amazing, especially the drawing room, library, cloisters, and chapel. It was hard to believe that this was to be my home for the next year—close enough to my home city to keep connections and distant enough to gather my thoughts away from temptation.

Meeting my fellow students that first day was a real eye-opener: an ex-miner from Nottinghamshire, a playwright from the Hebrides, and a black South African who had escaped the hideous apartheid regime in his country—there were accents from all corners of the UK. Pete from Burnley, Patrick from London, Bob from Alloa, Bruce from Stirling, and Jimmy from Glasgow. There was also Jacquetta, Sheila, and Elizabeth. Conversations that started tentatively are now in full swing. We were all vastly different but shared a mutual sense of failure at school.

As I looked around, I was awe-struck by our new learning environment: there was the drawing room—decorated around 1870—a 19th-century chapel, and a wood-panelled library filled with first editions—historical accounts, philosophies, political treatises, and great works of literature. Inspiration was built into the building's DNA, and each part of it revealed a treasure trove of artefacts and decorative flourishes.

My room was in an adjacent modern block with views across a great verdant expanse. After frenetic London, I was enjoying the sounds of bird songs, the whispering of breezes, and the rustling of leaves. I had arrived in a place where the challenges were intellectual. The clamour to survive had been supplanted by a desire to learn.

Where would it go?

I had no idea. But I was making friends from across the social and ethnic spectrum. Clifford and Sheila spoke in posh tones with a heightened volume. Northern Pete blushed with each soft utterance, while Bob's Clackmannanshire accent meant his words were rushed like a low-velocity machine gun. This was a human melting pot, and from the youngest at twenty-two to the oldest at sixty-five, we were about to share a life-changing adventure.

I picked up my guitar that evening, and as soon as the first chords were struck, I had attracted a small assembly in my room. Patrick, Bruce, Bob, Jimmy, and Patrick who brought his guitar and joined in. It was the perfect icebreaker—a bottle of wine was produced, and the conversation flowed as freely as the Burgundy we consumed. A knock on the door produced Alan, a late arrival from Sheffield who'd been held up by a delayed confirmation of his grant from South Yorkshire Council. My first impression was of a cheeky bastard who had broken the camaraderie of the evening.

I got used to Alan's forthright approach, and our friendship went on to endure the storms in our respective lives.

My first essay was a terrifying experience, but I somehow scrambled it together in time for the deadline. It was marked with a few complimentary and helpful comments. I was enjoying the learning immensely and found making friends with other students easy.

A few weeks after my arrival, there was a call for election to the Student Representative Council, for which I was persuaded to put my name forward. "Why me?" I couldn't figure out why anyone would see me as a prospect to speak on their behalf. I expected to lose the election, but I was wrong. I polled the highest number of votes and was duly elected to lead the SRC. This was a massive step for me, and I was still bewildered by my apparent popularity— especially given the diverse nature and range of experience of the students at Newbattle. I didn't see it then, but my travels in childhood and my recent experience on London's streets had endowed me with the ability to speak to anyone in any setting.

What Newbatttle was giving me was a bit like a rebirth. I had always been curious, but that curiosity had perversely been thwarted at school, where we were taught to order. I was learning about political constitutions and the essence of economics and beginning to appreciate the beauty and challenge of great literature. I was also learning how to hold an argument and use gentle persuasion rather than the sledgehammer anger that I had garnered to assert a position. I became a serial winner at Scrabble and a dismal disappointment at table tennis.

Sheila and I could not be more different in how we spoke, viewed the world, or in our backgrounds and expectations. Yet somehow, that contrast was like a magnet, and we became the most unlikely of lovers in those first few months. I took her to Edinburgh and gave her an insider's view of the city. We visited Dad and were treated to one of his culinary specialties. We browsed bookshops, sat in cafes, walked through woodlands, and talked well into the night. The relationship's intensity wasn't to last, but we had given each other a great deal in those early weeks.

In government and politics seminars, we discussed models of democracy and how the UK was governed from Westminster. These seminar discussions usually sparked conversations that lasted well into the wee hours of the morning. I was hearing the perspectives of Marxists, Maoists, and Trotskyists. I didn't like those dogmas because they all seemed to be packaged and labelled as complete.

I have never felt comfortable with any narrowing of the focus, and the problem with followers of political doctrines is that they lose the capacity to challenge their own beliefs because they are handed to them on a platter. "I am a Trotskyist" has a finality about it, and it allows people to escape from intellectual analysis. What does it really mean? I have yet to be given a calm and unprejudiced explanation.

Democracy is the most curious of all political concepts because those who purport to live by it are often the most dictatorial in their views. The UK may be a democracy, but I question its validity in practice. Polling turnouts (which are usually low) and the kind of representative structure we employ are flawed in so many ways. What I hear again and again is that it's better than a dictatorship. Being sold that notion over and over again leads us to a false complacency that's deeply damaging.

At Newbattle, we had intense political discussions, but I regularly found myself challenging entrenched political ideologues. My political position is always a work in progress and rarely aligned with the party system. Having found myself for a while in the wastelands of our society, I had seen how people were forced into behaviours that further alienated them from their society. Yet there was experience and resourcefulness in abundance among them.

I was to discover after I left Newbattle that real politics can start in homes and on the streets. The welfare state was born for the best of reasons, but over the years it has put a stranglehold on the lives of too many people who became frightened to rock the boat and lose their benefits. When I asked Nobel Prize winner Professor Mohammed Unis, who set up the Grameen (Micro Finance) Bank in Bangladesh, what he thought of the British welfare system, he said much the same thing: that it discourages people from playing a productive role in their community. It has been an intellectually weak approach that has seen the emergence of food banks around the country. Has it had a positive and galvanising impact on our poorer communities? No, it hasn't.

Newbattle was opening up conversations on these topics, and it was refreshing to be able to discuss them in a thoughtful and intelligent way. We were able to reflect on how our own personal lives had been affected by policies. The environment at the college was perfect for pensive contemplation in the Italian gardens, lush woods, and vast greenery—each giving one a sense of space and place.

CHAPTER 36

Now What?

At twenty-two years of age, I didn't fully appreciate what we had, but it was a real opportunity that only a lucky few were ever given. Almost all the others applied for a second year. I was restless and keen to get out into the world and use my sharpened mind to make my way. I'd proven to myself that I was as capable of studying and learning as anyone who had crossed an important bridge.

At college, Bruce, Bob, Alan, and I became very close companions during that year.

Bruce was a remarkable young man. An athlete at school in Stirling, he had developed rheumatoid arthritis, a horribly disabling and painful condition. Somehow Bruce kept defying the odds and always seemed to find ways to adapt his twisted body to cope with the rigours of life. He would routinely thrash me at table tennis and remind me daily of the huge capacity human beings have to conquer adversity.

Bob, an eccentric in true Celtic tradition, had his finger firmly pressed on the self-destruct button. When he drank, he did so excessively; when he backed a political cause, he did so wholeheartedly; and when he fell out with us, he took it to an extreme—camping alone in the woods for days. Despite that, he was a character whose company and wit I valued enormously. After Newbattle, he managed to combine two of his passions to great effect—weaponry and sheep rustling. The latter activity became his signature.

When the phone rang one morning at an absurdly early hour, I feared it was a family death. "Mike," came this whispered voice. "Have you got a van?" "You know I don't have a fucking van, Bob, and it's five in the morning." "I've killed a sheep on Arthur's Seat," he explained, "and I need a vehicle to move it." I slammed the phone down. Two days later, I saw Bob dragging a large sack into a Leith butcher's shop. "It's that sheep," he winked.

He then told me of his disappointment the evening before.

After years of sexual inactivity, he finally clicked with a woman from Northern Ireland and somehow managed to persuade her to come back to his flat. He asked her to put the kettle on while he emptied his bursting bladder. As he was undoing his fly, a piercing scream shattered the air, followed by a clatter of heels on the stairs. She had fled at a rate of knots. Bob still couldn't understand why the sight of a dead sheep bleeding into the kitchen sink might put a girl off.

When I took Bob to stay with my sister in the East Lothian village of West Saltoun that Christmas, he somehow found a bayonet blade from WWI in the folds of the settee, and I had to hold him back from an attack on the sheep in the field behind the house.

When my four nephews opened their gifts and found toy guns among the booty, Bob seized on the chance of a mock gun battle with them that seemed to rage on for hours—they loved Bob.

Alan was a different character altogether. Born in Leeds, his upbringing was strict, religious, and oppressive. Taking his first chance to escape, Alan moved to Sheffield and the steel industry, which was thriving at the time. Alan was talkative, friendly, and generous to a tee. He was and is passionate about educational opportunities for all. It was through his trade union that he was introduced to Newbattle, and he was in his element at the college. After two years there, he went on to study history at Nottingham University. Alan had an obsession with branded shampoos and conditioners and would spend endless hours washing his locks. "Have you tried this amazing conditioner?" he would say, excitedly pushing a bottle or tube in my direction. It all seemed so incongruous.

It was Alan who persuaded me to go to Sheffield with him after our year of college ended. He was to return in September, while I was now a free agent.

I liked Sheffield a lot. Here was one of the great wealth-creating cities, with its values firmly rooted in an egalitarian model. Buses were ubiquitous and cheap, with fewer cars. Sheffield was internationally renowned for its steel production and innovations like stainless steel.

I had learned at college that Sheffield was mentioned as early as the 14th century in Chaucer's Canterbury Tales for producing knives.

Like Glasgow, the city would suffer from a painful and quick industrial decline during the 70s and 80s, and like Glasgow, the city had been designed to give free enjoyment to its people—61% of Sheffield's entire area is green space, and a third of the city lies within the Peak District National Park.

Needing a job and money, it was a no-brainer that I would try the steelworks. The first stop was Daniel Doncaster's privately owned steel production plant near Hillsborough. I was taken on right away and started in a line that produced camshafts for Ford motors. My job was to grab the red-hot metal with a set of industrial-strength tongs and move it to the finishing production stage. I thought the ovens at the biscuit factory were hot. I had now moved into another league. Daniel Doncaster had been around since 1778 and was famed for its development of crucible steel-making in the manufacture of hand tools.

The job was tough and required strength and concentration.

Teamwork was critical—one mistake jeopardised production and endangered the lives of those around you. The experience of working with such a tight-knit team was a huge learning experience for me. When others depend on you, as they did at the Steelworks, you develop a heightened sense of responsibility. You never want to let anyone down, and you are always alert and ready if someone is injured or failing in the heat.

There was an Australian who worked alongside me who collapsed at his station. I knew that if I didn't step in and maintain both his and my stages of production, there would have been a dangerous pile-up. Somehow, I managed both our jobs while shouting for help. We became good friends after that, and he would return to my flat after a backshift. We'd open a few beers and talk about life and politics. His perspective on international politics was intriguing. Coming from Australia, he saw the UK as a mother ship that his country was inextricably tied to. Although Australia had been granted independence in 1931, he told me that Australian acts of Parliament still needed royal assent from our queen. He was right, and it wasn't until 1986 that Australia's real political independence came into force.

Again, I thought of how democracy can never work if real decision-making is impenetrable.

In my life, I have seen the enormous surge of energy and confidence that follows when people feel they have a real stake in shaping their future. I didn't know it then, but that principle played a huge part in my life and work.

We have a tradition in the UK of breeding and educating our officer class. When people go straight into management and know little of the industry, they tend to look disdainfully at the workers. Yet in the steelworks industry, I saw amongst my co-workers an enormous knowledge of the industry and ways to improve it. Steelworkers like miners and shipbuilders would have a right battle in the years to come.

Early in 1973, I hung up my insulated gloves and returned to Edinburgh. My arm muscles were bulging and not needed at the University of Edinburgh, where I was working on indexing with Professor Nickolaisan on Scottish place names. It may not have been the highest-ranked post at the university, but I learned a lot in those three months. I was dying to tell my Fife friends that Auchtermuchty meant "Hollow of the Pigs".

Pat, a blonde-haired Irishman with horn-rimmed glasses and narrow, pinched features, arrived in my life through my father. When he was introduced, I was taken aback by the strength of his handshake grip. On the outside, Pat was a man you would expect to see working behind a library desk, yet he was steely and strong. He was ex-Army. I was to learn that he was strong to the core.

Everything about him seemed contradictory: he was a painter, a meditator, and a warrior of the wild. I liked him enormously.

After a few sojourns to Sandy Bell's Bar, where fiddlers, guitarists, and banjo players would jam day and night, Pat had a bolt from the blue suggestion for me. "I'm a youth worker at the YWCA", he said, "and I know there's a call out for someone to run the Children's Summer Playscheme in Craigentinny this year." "Me? Look after a bunch of children for the summer"? I threw my head back in laughter. It seemed like a preposterous suggestion. I'd never been in charge of anyone before, and the idea of keeping thirty or more kids occupied for days on end seemed a stretch well beyond my experience. Pat said, "I think you'd be good at it." I was taken aback. Nothing in my experience would indicate that. Had Pat seen something, I was missing? " When he asked me about my own childhood and the impact that adults in various settings had made on my wellbeing and confidence, I began to see that it was what I had learned as a child that I could offer as experience.

I said I would think about it and returned to my drink.

Lying in bed, I couldn't sleep that night as the idea rolled over and over in my mind. Could I really take on that responsibility? I recalled the awful teachers I had encountered throughout my schooling and how very few had left me with any sense of self-worth. Damn it. They were trained and qualified to teach children. If I was ever going to prove that there were better ways to engage young people, I should jump at this chance. I had been off the drugs for a long time now; I was healthy and had proven myself a hard worker. And if I was to keep stretching to new challenges, there was surely no distance too far for me.

I said yes to taking charge of the emotional and physical welfare of children aged five to twelve for up to six weeks during that summer. Parents would entrust me with their children—if I could make a success of this, it would be the single greatest triumph in my life so far.

CHAPTER 37

Unleashing the Power of People

I woke with a headache and a slight shiver that morning, but I had a job to do, and nothing would hold me back—certainly not a head cold. When I arrived at the school, I met Louise, a fifteen-year-old who was to be my volunteer helper. She was looking to me for guidance and instruction. Fifteen minutes later, we had acquired thirty-five children—all expectant and excited. I felt a surge of responsibility, and as I surveyed these little faces, the immensity of the task hit me.

I would have to draw on all my knowledge and experience if I was to make this a success. I grabbed a small rubber ball from a basket full of assorted toys and threw it to one little girl; she caught it adeptly. "Tell us your name and then throw it to someone else, and they will do the same." They all laughed and quickly entered into the spirit of the game. Ten minutes later, I knew that they were with me. The real challenge was going to be keeping them in the same high spirits for the weeks ahead. I determined that they would learn something from the experience—something they didn't get in the classroom.

I was given a list of trips and activities provided by the council that we could sign the youngsters in our charge up for. These were children at ages when choice was not common currency. That didn't seem fair, so I decided to put these to a majority vote and find an advocate for each activity.

After a set of exhausting physical games, they were ready for a sit-down and a chat. The older girls had already decided that Louise and I were great marriage material—rather than show irritation or embarrassment, we played along with it and enjoyed the daily whistling and banter. I remembered how often, in my childhood, my enthusiasm and laughter had been quelled by adult dampeners.

I divided the room into different activities and got each of the children to agree to try something they had never done. It was magic, and by the time I got home, I was shattered. On route, I had made a few purchases for an idea I had for the following day. Making percussive musical instruments from plant potholders, wallpaper paste, greaseproof paper, and an assortment of scraps proved to be a winner with the kids, and we ended up with a mini and very Celtic version of a Brazilian Samba band. This was many years before this country's love affair with percussion bands. Any exercise that allows humans to create something of value and then use it is great learning. I remember making a watch stand in woodwork in school and how utterly futile it felt. Who uses a watch stand, for goodness sake?

Over the next few weeks, we kept the children having fun, learning, and taking responsibility for different elements of our programme. We took trips to beaches, woods, museums, and the zoo. I saw some of them make huge leaps in confidence as the weeks progressed. When it came to the end of that summer and saying goodbye, it was with a heavy heart. Some of them clearly lived in homes where they had low priority with their parents. I saw the impact this was having on young lives. There were the physical manifestations: swollen eyes, bruised arms, and torn clothing. And yet there was a deeper hurt I could see. I did what I did during the time they spent with me in order to lift their spirits and give them a boost to their self-belief.

187

After a few intermittent relationships, I met Arlene—a classical violinist with extraordinary talent and a primary school teacher to boot. We talked for hours and agreed on so much that we almost lost ourselves in our enthusiasm. My recent experience of running a playscheme resonated with her and belied my outward image as a physical kind of guy. There was also a strong physical chemistry between us, and I had a feeling that this relationship would endure a few storms. Above all, we were bound by the potential of a musical duo.

Arlene made me quickly realise how limited my musical skills were. She was classically trained, while I was self-taught and wholly intuitive. She was just what I needed in my life and remains to this day the one and only girlfriend with whom I could combine my music. As adept as she was as a classical musician, I was astonished at how quickly she was able to pick up on Celtic and American country fiddling. Within a few days, we had established a whole set we could play together. It was electrifying, and I couldn't wait to step on stage with her and blast out our new songs. It didn't take long to get a few gigs under our belts. Every non-working hour was now spent with Arlene, and we became highly productive—feeding off each other's ideas, creating new music, and developing new arts and crafts challenges for her pupils at school. I was now able to offer a wee bit of expertise based on my playscheme experience because I had figured out how to make a variety of percussive instruments from all sorts of household and natural materials. I was even asked by the city's theatre workshop to run some sessions for adult leaders and children.

What a remarkable turnaround for me!

Pat called and invited me to a meeting with his boss at the YWCA. Mitzi was American, beautiful, and very bright. When I met her in her Bruntsfield flat, I was excited and slightly intimidated at the same time—she carried herself with such glamour and sophistication. With a cup of coffee in hand, I began to relax into our discussion. "Mike", she said, "Pat is leaving us, so we need someone to take over the running of our small community facility in Lochend—we see this as a community hub and a place from which we have a chance to connect with and positively involve local people. Would you be interested in taking on that role?" I almost choked on my biscuit. "Me?" "Yes, Michael, you. I have heard so much about you, and I think you would be ideal—in any case, it's a chance for you to make your mark professionally."

This was an extraordinary offer,and I couldn't refuse it. In any case, if I am honest, the opportunity to work with Mitzi created so many fantasies in my mind that I would have accepted almost any task she assigned me.

"Yes, I'd love to Mitzi, and I promise I won't let you down". Financial arrangements and a start date were agreed upon, and I bounced out into Bruntsfield Place with a smile that took days to wipe off. I had the opportunity to make my mark on people's lives. Having lived on the edge for so long and skipped through so many jobs, my work record didn't warrant this level of responsibility, but I had shown during the summer that I had something to offer. This is just what I craved, and I wanted to make something of it.

Lochend is an inner-city council estate with a multiplicity of social problems and the pervasive influence of low aspiration. I wanted to use my experience to show others that anything is possible. My first target was to resurrect a youth club that had been running but had been allowed to slide. Using posters, walking the streets, and chatting to young people, I managed to assemble a group of lads that looked and sounded to me like the local gang. It turned out that they were.

Over the coming weeks, I got closer to them and started to plan activities with them. They wanted to form a football team and join a league. So, we agreed that a series of fundraising opportunities were necessary to fuel this ambition with new strips, balls, and all the other accoutrements of team football. The next day, they turned up carrying various bundles in their arms. Is that for a jumble sale?

I inquired enthusiastically. Naw, they said, we've got all the stuff we need. As they emptied a series of bags, it was clear that they had managed to acquire a full set of brandnew strips. "How did you manage that?" "We nicked them from a store."

"Heavens above. That's not fucking right," I said with a horrified look. But I was hiding my admiration for their enterprise, and if I was being true to myself, this wasn't too far from my own acts of dishonesty. They didn't want to let me down, so they acted quickly and decisively without the needless process of fundraising. I wonder how things would have developed between us if I had marched them up to the shop and asked them to come clean and apologise. I didn't. But I did ask for no more antics like that under my watch. The football team was then formed, and the stolen strips were on display in local parks every Saturday.

I felt I had achieved a lot in that job, especially in engaging local young people, stretching them beyond their comfort zone, and creating in them a greater sense of their own power to make things happen. I had tapped into the resourcefulness and leadership potential they already had and felt sure that they would go on and do well. Threatening as they were to begin with, I treated them with respect and pushed them to exceed their own expectations. In turn, I earned their respect by showing that I wasn't to be messed with. My time in building and steel work had toughened me up considerably.

In 1995, more than twenty years later, I spotted the gang leader pushing a wheelchair into Easter Road Stadium. When I asked what he was doing now, he got really animated and told me how he had formed and now ran a disabled basketball team that travelled around to competitions.

I knew then that those qualities I had spotted in him all those years ago had been there in abundance. When I gave him and the others responsibility and trust, they rose to it, which I had done as well. I had learned something of incalculable value: never underestimate people's capacity to reach extraordinary heights. I also learned that I was good under pressure.

After a few months, I saw a job advertisement placed by Craigmillar Festival Society (a housing estate in the south of Edinburgh), which was a locally run organisation with a focus on the arts as a community development tool. I knew of Helen Crummy, the remarkable woman who had set up the organisation. Helen was one of Craigmillar's first residents in 1931, when her family moved to the estate. What prompted Helen's activism was a simple question asked at her son's primary school in 1962. Her request was a humble one: "Can my son be taught the violin?" He replied by telling her that it took the school all of its time to teach these children the 'three R's'. So, Helen joined a local mother's group that had decided to show how talented their children were and started the Craigmillar Festival Society. That story gave a lie to the notion of education as an equal opportunity. This was a generation of children deemed incapable because of their geographical location.

When I met Helen for an interview, I was struck by the contrast between her quiet demeanour and her passionate and determined purpose. We hit it off immediately, and after a lengthy and sometimes emotional chat, I was offered the job as a neighbourhood worker. Right from the outset, I was involved in a production, preparing for the annual Craigmillar Festival. Directed by Sandy Neilson, a top theatre and TV director. The production featured a combination of seasoned actors and locals taking to the stage for the first time.

I was blown away by the quality of the performance.

Joan Bakewell hosted a TV documentary on the work that was being done in Craigmillar. This was an imaginative attempt to subvert the cycle of expected failure. With some local performers graduating into professional actors, there was proof of a rich seam of talent in the community. I knew from my own experience of the enormous untapped talent that exists in the most unexpected of places.

People can be extraordinary when given a chance to test and express their talents. If mine weren't even on the radar at school, how many other people like me would have left education with their confidence undernourished?

Those who experience things firsthand know best. When, as leaders, we learn that and live by it, we have uncovered the secret of success.

CHAPTER 38

Oh Baby

After a few weeks with the Craigmillar Festival Society, I was given another exciting opportunity—to track the preparation of the society's newspaper. This meant spending a week in Glasgow with the printer and learning how to plate and then offset print the job. I loved the smells and sounds of the print presses, and that process from laying out the words and images through to the finished production excited me. Seeing freshly inked copies flying off the printer in large numbers and then holding in your hand the results of your efforts and knowing that thousands would then do the same was thrilling. I loved moving typeset columns into position, creating headlines, and pasting photographic images onto blank pages.

Just as I was settling into my role at the Festival Society, Arlene dropped a bombshell on me. "I am pregnant," she said. "But you are on the pill!" I gasped.

I don't know why, but this announcement and its timing terrified me. I sat that night and tried to figure out how Arlene and I could bring up a child and give it the kind of security that I craved during childhood. The last thing I wanted was to fail a child, and I simply wasn't ready. My mood plummeted, and I went into a deep depression—my depressive qualities had surfaced before, and I managed to keep them from people close to me. This time, I felt out of control. It wasn't the last time I experienced what it's like to feel that level of despair and hopelessness. It hit me like a hurricane, sweeping me so far off course that I almost took my own life. I was taken into the Royal Edinburgh Hospital again—this time for psychological analysis and treatment. For days, I could only look at the walls, and it took a monumental effort by the staff to get me to attend therapy sessions.

Arlene never came to see me. She had admitted that the pregnancy story was a fabrication designed to test my commitment to her. When I was eventually discharged, I went to see her and found her with another man. It was horrible. I felt my life dissembling before me. Too embarrassed to own up to my depression, I left the Craigmillar Festival Society and spent the next few weeks in recovery. I took refuge for a few weeks in Nunraw, a Cistercian monastery just outside Haddington. The simplicity of life there removed me from all the pressures that had been building up in the previous weeks.

When I first arrived, I would sit for hours looking into space.

Father Benedict, who ran the guesthouse, slowly started to engage me. He was in his seventies and only slept two hours a night—something he put down to a clear conscience. I tried to contemplate what it would be like to feel free of guilt but found the whole notion impossible. I was not and will never be religious, so I never attended any services. I knew that I had to find my own meaning of life to allow myself the luxury of self-forgiveness. What he did was ask some simple questions. With each prompt, he drew out of me a part of the complex picture I had built of the world and myself. When depression hits, it's like a tsunami—you feel yourself drowning and lose your natural instincts.

With Father Benedict, I started talking of the children at the youth club I had led and the feeling of achievement I got from seeing youngsters do something they hadn't believed was in their realm of possibility. He got me to acknowledge that I have much to give. That slow realisation gave me a little more strength each day. I was feeling a little better. In a surreal moment, Brother Frances turned up in my room with a guitar and a Simon and Garfunkel songbook in hand. We got on really well. He brought with him such an air of serenity that I felt lightheaded. By the time I returned to Edinburgh, I had recovered my equilibrium and seemed to have acquired a new appetite for life.

CHAPTER 39

Young Volunteer Force

It was one of those glorious autumn days in the city, and the Meadows were a montage of nature's most glorious colours—amber, gold, orange, rust, terracotta, and yellow. As the leaves pirouetted around me, I felt a surge of energy and optimism. I was ready to work again and in earnest. This adrenaline rush and the need to act overcame me. That summer, I played at a festival in this very place and drew a great reception from the swelled crowd. Without Arlene, I was creating powerful performances. This felt like my domain. I had stood on stage here, and I had conquered it. I was playing a few gigs, but I was lousy at self-promotion and didn't have much time for agents. I needed to be captivated by a purpose—whatever I did, it would have to be about people.

When I saw an advertisement by an organisation called the Young Volunteer Force, based in London, calling for three community workers to set up a project in Leith, I was excited by the prospect of making a real impact on that part of the city that for too long had been allowed to deteriorate. Although the job asked for qualifications I didn't have, I had some real-life experience that I felt would bring energy and ideas to the job. When I posted the application, I looked to the skies—please let this be successful. The longer I waited for a response, the less I believed in my chances.

Then, out of the blue, I received a phone call and an invitation to attend an interview. Seated before a professional interview panel for the first time should have been daunting, but I came alive during that half-hour, answering questions with measured enthusiasm and clarity. With each idea I mentioned, eyebrows would raise, and notes were taken. Surely, I had done enough to get a chance.

When the offer of the job came through, I was ecstatic. Here was a chance to set up a project from scratch and make things happen. I knew the area of Leith in which our focus was to be. Densely populated tenement streets with no running hot water, only a kitchen sink to wash, and an outside toilet. It is hard to believe that in the mid-seventies, so much of our housing stock was still lacking even the most rudimentary of facilities. I also knew that many residents lived in poverty and in the precarious grip of private landlords.

We had a significant spending budget and a blank sheet of paper to work from—we were expected to create valuable learning for use in other similar urban areas. No pressure!

My skills were in finding ways to engage residents (most were in privately rented homes) and get their active backing and involvement. It was a huge challenge to overturn the belief that people's destinies were set in concrete. Here was a group of young people with a message of hope for something better. Slowly, that message began to take hold among a small group of locals, ready to step up, learn, and take a leadership role in their community. Fraught with challenges, bureaucratic blocks, and preconditions, we managed to establish a local housing association able to purchase properties, take them into community ownership, and renovate them from top to bottom. It was exhilarating to see plans take shape, architect's drawings being presented to local people, and the first completed refurbishment.

As we worked with people locally, it became clear that community life was not just about where people lived but also how they lived.

They wanted their kids to have hope, opportunity, and real prospects; they wanted to ensure that older people had opportunities to meet, have fun, and get the nutrition they needed. Local people were becoming almost statesmanlike as they stood and talked of new hope at public meetings or as representatives attending council meetings. It was a magical time, and each day, as I was imparting my experience, I was also learning new skills.

We did so much during those years.

Leith is an area of Edinburgh that was once a prosperous port in its own right.

Leith now has four Michelin-starred restaurants, a plethora of international and seafood restaurants, and great delis and gastro bars. It would have taken a visionary with a twisted mind to have predicted that in the mid-seventies, when it was still a bit of a no-go area. I love this area and its people and now regard it as my home.

There is something distinctive about Leith. It shows a healthy disdain for status and order and is always ready to extend the hand of friendship, regardless of race or religion.

I would describe Leith now as Scotland's Greenwich Village— creative and full of possibility. I could never have predicted just how much of a role Leith would play in my life in the years to come.

The Young Volunteer Force (now renamed the Community Projects Foundation) had projects the length and breadth of Britain, with some great people working around the country and at HQ. At the first annual conference, I met them all. It was a fantastic experience, and whatever I did, I must have made an impression.

I was approached to represent Scotland and the North of England in the Trade Union (ASTMS)—an invitation I duly accepted. It meant more travel to and from London, but I didn't mind that. How different it was to arrive in the capital in a British Rail sleeper, step off that train, and head off into London's busy streets filled with important purpose.

Within two months, I had been elected National Shop Steward—an extraordinary and mystifying elevation. I was finding it hard to see what it was that people saw in me that made them want me to speak on their behalf.

At HQ, I met Jeremy, one of the poshest people I had ever known. There was so much confidence about him that my natural instincts kicked in and I felt slightly cowed. Yet, we talked one evening well into the night and got on so well that he invited me to his home for the weekend. His wife, who would later become a highly successful novelist, and his children were warm with their welcome. They had invited guests to dinner that evening who were apparently really looking forward to meeting me. Billy Connelly, who had recently captivated millions of TV viewers during his appearance on the Michael Parkinson show, was one of the main topics of conversation. They loved Billy and the way he had brought the richness of working-class Glasgow humour to a wider audience.

I told a few stories at the dinner table and held the guests in thrall—it seemed that a Scot was now very much in demand. Later that weekend, Jeremy asked if I would speak about what I was doing in Leith to an audience of business and public service leaders at the Institute of Cultural Arts in the Pall Mall. I agreed, then started to worry—would they understand me? Would they take to my provocative messages around alienation?

I was a quivering wreck when I arrived at this grand building in Central London, especially when I realised that just a few years before, I had slept a night in the neighbouring doorway, been unceremoniously kicked awake by a Met (metal-toed) boot, and moved on.

What a remarkable journey I had been on!

Now people were gathering in this great, pillared room to hear me speak. I decided to tell them about my nocturnal experience next door. That was it. They were captivated from the start. I took them from seriousness to laughter and then back again. The applause I received at the end told me that I had pulled it off. As people milled about me and asked me questions, I realised that what I had that many didn't was the experience of mental and physical struggle and the ability to articulate what I had learned.

CHAPTER 40

Next

The relationship with Arlene had drained me, and although I had enjoyed a few fleeting relationships with women—one had chased me home with an axe and another had sprung at me from behind a tree—I felt ready for a more serious relationship.

Your own father's birthday party is not where you would normally expect to meet a new lover—for all sorts of reasons that require no explanation. When Dad told me he had invited a girl he thought I would like, my feigned indifference masked an inner excitement. I was willing to yield to his judgement more than anyone else's. Yet I had also learned that disappointment could follow eager anticipation. His rider was that she has some sort of friendship with a guy named Laurie, which put me on red alert.

Her hair was a dismembered haystack, her face diminished by this auburn explosion—yet I was captivated by its lightly freckled pallor, aquiline shape, and lively eyes. She was pre-Raphaelite in her appearance, and there was a slight awkwardness about her demeanour—her feet pointed inwards as she struggled to compose herself—not fully comfortable in her own skin. "This is the Winifred I've heard so much about." My voice broke the silence and carried all the assurance of the life-worn twenty-six-year-old I was. "How are you?" There may have been many more words spoken with eloquence, but I can't remember any details. What I knew was that here was the woman I had craved for so long. I had to speak to Laurie and ask him about the status of his relationship with her. Nothing could stand in our way. I found an excuse to leave her company for a moment and found him. I tried to stay cool and calm. "Laurie, what's the situation with you and Winfred?" "Oh, nothing really; we're just friends." My heart leapt with joy at those words. "So, she's free?" I had to double-check. Before he finished his affirmative reply, I was back at her side and able to take a more serious look. She was beautiful and slim, and I could see the intelligence in her eyes.

I saw my father smile encouragingly. We talked until the small hours, and when the guests streamed out, we were lying in an embrace. My hand began to explore the back of her neck, and I tried a few tentative strokes. "I'd better go before we ruin the evening," she said. I was so glad she had that maturity. I didn't want this to be another notch on my bedpost.

We agreed to meet again and kissed. I was ecstatic, and when I eventually slept that night, it was with a broad smile on my face. I was happy.

The next day, we met in town for a coffee and a stroll around the shops. Christmas was approaching, and the frosted pavements glimmered with the reflections of an assortment of brightly coloured lights in the shop windows. It was cold, but every part of me warmed to Winifred. I was captivated by her looks, her intelligence, and her gentle sense of humour.

There are times in your life when you feel such a surge of exhilaration that it's difficult to contain the emotion. That's what it felt like that day—as though a precious gift had been presented to me. I felt alive and happy. Things were falling into place for me. I experienced a feeling of completeness I had never known. No path crossed is ever without obstacles. I arrived for dinner the next evening wearing a crisp white shirt, and it was like a magnet to the plate of spaghetti bolognese she served up. Perhaps being shirtless for the next few hours was the perfect icebreaker, and we found ourselves in bed later that evening.

Life with Winifred was always interesting and exciting. When I met her parents and sisters, any anxieties I might have had about my integration into their family life were quickly assuaged.

When I moved in with Winifred, her father Alex, and her sister Lucy, I felt our lives would be forever intertwined. I was happy. I was working hard in Leith, and she was doing well at the University of Edinburgh. With my lack of educational success, I was at times intimidated by her success at university. I still had a chip on my shoulder, and I hated myself for it.

As settled as we were, she had finished her university course and was now in the job market. For a while, she worked as part-time childminder and part-time waitress in a seafood restaurant. Life was good, but the funding was coming to an end for my job. I had learned through experience how to put words and images together and paste up posters, magazines, leaflets, and posters. Nothing excited me more than the delivery of a fresh print—seeing my own artwork brought to life, touching it, sniffing it, and rubbing it against my cheek. It was reinforcement of my belief that producing things and doing what we enjoy can be an elixir of life. I created a couple of exhibitions using some wildly unconventional items and won an award for one such invention. I was being creative and getting paid for it.

I wanted more of the same.

Sneaking a look at Napier College's prospectus, I noticed a Communication Studies course, which included journalism, advertising, media, English, art, and design—there was also the chance to learn how to type. I looked again and again at the details, and while I didn't have the entry qualifications, I really wanted to do it. It sounded so exciting, I wanted to weep. Winifred wasn't so keen. It would mean a loss of income at a time when she wanted to establish some security and independence from her family.

I was in a dilemma.

This was an opportunity to build on what I had learned for myself and widen my options. I called the college to explain my situation. If I was accepted as a mature student, I was told, relevant experience could be counted and entry qualifications waived. Surely now I should go for it, and I did.

By early summer I heard that I had been accepted. After being chucked out of school at fifteen, I was now about to start college for the second time. I was twenty-nine now, and I was ready for it. After her initial reluctance, Winifred was pleased for me. I vowed to get decorating jobs and earn enough money to make up for the loss of income we would incur. Her anxieties were understandable. Her dad was on the verge of selling his house, and she and I would have to move into rented accommodation.

After getting a foothold in Stockbridge and getting to know so many small shopkeepers and local personalities, I wanted to stay in the area, and so did Winifred. Her life had centred around that area, and so many of her friends and work connections were within a square mile. We didn't have to wait too long or travel very far—Danube Street was just around the corner, and long-term friend Kay Butcher, on hearing of our plight, offered us a large room in her three-story Georgian house.

From our enormous bay window, we had views across the cobbled street and straight onto what must have been the most prestigious brothel in the country. 17a Danube Street was a legendary brothel run by Madam Dora Noyce, who described the establishment in court as "a YMCA with extras." Dora certainly knew what side her bread was buttered on and would come around local doors raising money for the Deep-Sea Fishermen. It has been said in a lighthearted vein that the brothel's busiest time was during the General Assembly of the Church of Scotland—I can confirm that as true. A simple body count indicated that men in the church were not averse to a night out with a twist. The brothel would offer us hours and hours of entertainment. From the brazen to the surreptitious, it was a fascinating study in human (well, male) behaviour. Some arrived in large cars with shadowed windows, while others would walk around the block a few times before plucking up the courage.

A social anthropologist from Edinburgh University bought it after Dora's death, and the business closed down. He told us that in one room there was a bed, a cot, and a bookcase—only one book was there "How to Win Friends and Influence People", by Dale Carnegie. I saw it as an interesting social commentary on our times. One day I wanted to write a definitive book like that, but I had a lot of learning to do. I was thirsting to do so, yet Napier College was looming on the horizon.

That summer, I worked all the hours I could find on decorating jobs that came through friends and connections. I did regular twelve-hour shifts and once worked continuously for eighteen hours to get a restaurant finished in time for a reopening. It was bringing money in, and on the cusp of starting college, it felt good to have some cash in my pocket. I also played a few paid gigs, and by the time I was due to start college, I felt secure about my ability to supplement my student grant and make the most of the opportunity.

I was now in my early thirties, and with Winifred, I was enjoying the most settled period in my life. I was also beginning to think long-term. When a rundown basement flat became available for sale, we snapped it up. It really did need everything done to it though. For the first time since early childhood, I felt I had a home.

I saw us being together forever and positively revelled in our newfound home-comforts.

After I completed my college course with a Higher National

Diploma and a distinction, I worked for a couple of years in community education.

I received a phone call from a friend who invited me to apply for a job. She was involved in establishing a new, Glasgow-based organisation–eventually it would morph into the Wise Group as it expanded its services and reach. Its aim is to help the long-term unemployed back into work by doing vital and valuable works around the city.

I knew from the outset that I wanted to be involved. I was invited to apply for the position of head of marketing. It was felt I had the enthusiasm, energy, and skills to be able to spread the word about the benefits of Heatwise (I coined the name) to locals, in a language they would understand, and to encourage them to get involved. When I got the job that's exactly what I did.

Commuting daily between Edinburgh and Glasgow was taking its toll and I took a flat share for a couple of days a week. Winifred was understandably unhappy and tensions began to develop. When I heard that my dad had suffered a heart attack, I phoned Winifred and told her I would get the first train back. Astonishingly, she told me that I should leave it to the following day. I didn't. My dad's life was in danger. After a trip to the hospital, I returned home. Winifred had a candlelit dinner prepared. I knew it wasn't meant for me, and that I had skewered her plans for the evening.

I said nothing and returned to Glasgow the following morning in a state of shell shock. My dad had narrowly escaped death and Winifred was seeing someone else. I felt myself plunging again. All the old demons were flexing their muscles. Winifred and I had been together for over ten years, and I knew I would be bereft. It was heart wrenching to separate from Winifred and leave the home we had built together. So much of us was invested in that little basement flat.

I saw her once more. It was a final plea.

Never again have we set eyes on each other.

I was thirty-six years-old, even though I had some serious relationships to this point in my life, I never again moved in with anyone. Five years later I enrolled at Glasgow Caledonian University for a Master of Business Administration (MBA) degree (part-time) and I started to think about business opportunities. Above all, I was a good communicator and so it made sense that my business should be in that field. I continued at my job until the right opportunity came along.

I attended a lecture on Risk by Professor Lisabeth May Kanter of Harvard Business School who talked about risk taking in life and business.

It occurred to me that my entire life had been influenced by risk.

I went into work the following morning and handed in my notice. It was a shock to my colleagues who tried to get me to reconsider but I told them my mind was made up.

My Dad was delighted when I called to let him know I'd be moving back to Edinburgh and that I planned to start my own business.

The following day I started to put my plans into action. Two days later, I phoned dad again. He was heading off to the Melrose Sevens (Rugby) tournament in the Borders with his new wife, Christine. I agreed to join them at their Edinburgh flat for dinner later that evening. This was to celebrate my new venture.

I drove to Edinburgh and visited my mum beforehand for a cup of tea and a chat. While I was there a call came through from Tony who told us that on the way back, Dad had had a heart attack in the car and that he'd died. I picked Tony up and we drove down to Borders General Hospital and met Christine in the reception area.

My dad was 74 years-old and his death was a huge shock to all of us. He was fit, regularly taking long walks in the Pentland Hills, and young in outlook. For most of my adulthood I thought of him more as a friend than a parent. His death made me think about my own life and it convinced me I'd made the right decision about quitting my job. It was time for me to stop running.

It was time to come home.

My mother died at the age of ninety. Tony was her major caregiver over many years. She dealt with Alzeimhers for ten years before she died. Brian lives in Australia, so Eileen and I helped out as much as we could. I enjoyed many hours sitting with her laughing and reminiscing. When she let me know that she wanted to go back to Egypt before she died, I managed to take her there five years before she passed away. It was a defining fortnight for me, seeing life through her eyes.

CHAPTER 41

Job Security

I find it odd to be arriving at the final chapter of my memoir when I was barely into my forties, but looking back from the vantage point of my 74th year, it seems to me that that's when my life proper really began. It was at that stage that I started to gain some genuine insight into the patterns of my behaviour and the influences that had allowed me to be, for so many years, at the mercy of circumstance.

Deliberately, I don't describe myself as having been a victim of circumstance or of anything else, for that matter, because I don't regard myself as such. I remain convinced I've always been responsible for my own destiny, albeit not always in control of it, and, while my past is chequered, with perhaps more lows than highs, I have no one other than myself to blame for those low points.

Accepting responsibility became imperative for me when I recognised that only by doing so could I move forward.

I recognise the damage done to my body through drug taking, but I feel I suffered more from violence, the break-up of my family, the physical privations I experienced sleeping rough on the streets, and mental illness. I suffered from what I now recognise as depression at a time when society and the medical profession were less equipped to deal with its consequences. They undoubtedly had a damaging effect on my life, professionally and personally, particularly in my ability to forge lasting and meaningful relationships.

All of those things taught me vital lessons that would make me a happier and more rounded adult. They made me aware of the importance of initiative and self-reliance and that only I could change my direction of travel. They showed me how my life could improve by being ambitious and having a positive attitude. They also revealed to me that the most important thing for me was not the size of my wage packet, the power I wielded at work, or the car I drove, but the influence that my behaviour could have on the lives of others and the sense of satisfaction I felt at the end of each day when my head hit the pillow, knowing that I had done the right thing.

My experiences of living on the streets, working in factories and at building sites, and living from hand-to-mouth also provided me with the source material for a new career as an adviser and speaker. I'd sunk deeper than most people ever do, and as a result, I'd developed resilience to the slings and arrows of life in a way that would prove very useful to me in the world of business. I discovered that, similar to the effects of aversion therapy, when you're confronted with extreme situations, the everyday challenges of life and work just don't seem all that daunting.

My generation of baby boomers was lucky in that we were virtually guaranteed a job for life. We took a degree or embarked on an apprenticeship, and we were assured that our trade or profession would provide us with gainful employment until we retired. We grew up in a world when governments strived to achieve full employment—when everyone who wanted a full-time job could have one and when job security was assumed. Joblessness was rare in the post-war years and regarded as an anachronism from the 1930s. It was an era when society was literally being rebuilt from the ground up. When there was so much work to do, it was never considered that there would not be jobs for everyone for years to come or that, having become skilled in a particular job, you would have assured employment until you decided otherwise.

While many of us today might feel envious of such job security, the problem was that a good number of the positions were mundane and functionary. It says a lot about such jobs that many of them have since been mechanised or overridden. The generations that performed conveyor-belt tasks had little or no requirement for critical decision-making and could also justifiably resent being replaced by robots and computers. Those jobs did little to encourage a spirit of loyalty or ambition, other than perhaps a determination to escape. When you're performing a single function that requires no creative input, there's little incentive to do the job better, only to do it as well as the task requires. They created a culture of working that was reactive and process-centered, in which the default of workers was to ask, "How little can I get away with?" rather than "What can I do to improve my performance?"

It could be argued that little has changed other than the fact that there is now less certainty of employment.

So how can we possibly navigate our way through this maze if we can't even be sure that the job we've decided on will exist in ten or even five years' time? How can we map a career path and plan for the future when we can take so little for granted? Well, my belief is that this new world order is actually a blessing, and it creates for young people amazing opportunities to extend their horizons, learn multiple new skills, and become more creative, adaptable, and intuitive than any generation in history.

As far back as the 1980s, I travelled to Scandinavia with The Wise Group, a Glasgow-based social enterprise that devises strategies for getting people who are long-term unemployed back to work. As a guest of the Danish Government, I learned that apart from valuing their health and their leisure time more than we do, Danes don't see themselves as having a lifelong career. They see their lives as lateral as well as longitudinal, and at any stage, personal satisfaction is as important as professional fulfilment.

They don't see themselves as being on a career ladder with the aim of reaching the top, but rather on a series of parallel conveyor belts from which they can switch whenever they want to. It's much more commonplace in Scandinavia to see people switch professions. For lawyers to become politicians or teachers to become truck drivers, for doctors to become farmers, and for plumbers to become librarians. Such moves are not regarded as regressive or punitive because they have a different view of careers, where life experience is seen as an asset and skills are more transferable. The notion of 'serving your time' in a particular trade or profession or landing a job because it's your turn is seen as contrary and un-meritocratic.

I now make my living through words, and I read at least two challenging works of fiction every week, but learning how to use language wasn't easy. It took me a number of years before I was able to convince myself that, not only did I enjoy using words constructively, I was really rather good at it.

From an early age, I could always tell a good story, but put a pen in my hand, and I froze. At school, this inhibited me to the point of paralysis. I felt increasingly alienated from my own language, which hindered me in every other subject. Much of this was the fault of my teachers and an education system that valued the formal structure of language above creativity and individualism. It wanted round pegs for its round holes and had neither the time, resources, nor inclination to understand square pegs like me.

The turning point for me came when I was encouraged to write as I spoke. Having been raised in Fife, with its rich, peculiar dialects and accents, I'd always been encouraged by teachers to regard the way my friends, neighbours, and family spoke as 'not proper English' and therefore as illegitimate. My schooling perpetuated the delusion that spoken and written communication were entirely separate. Now, across the UK, there are movements aimed at recognising and celebrating the value of regional speech. What used to be dismissed as 'slang' is now valued for its authenticity and diversity. Poetry, fiction, film, art, music, and cuisine that reflect the richness and values of their distinct localities are feted more than those that are regarded as 'mainstream'. The movement away from centralised political institutions is, I believe, motivated by the same impulses that have prompted the growth of microbreweries and the slow food movement.

I don't want young people to suffer from language deprivation in the same way I did for much of my early life. Attitudes toward the teaching of language in schools are now changing, but not quickly enough.

Dialect and authenticity should be celebrated for their richness rather than regarded as signs of low worth. We can only appreciate language properly by reading, and we should never lose sight of that. I believe genuinely and passionately that nothing excites the imagination like the written word.

Confidence comes from a greater understanding and realisation of our strengths and qualities. We come to recognise that we have the intellectual power to influence things and people around us in lots of different ways. I've found no greater motivation to better myself than through reading and the use of language.

CHAPTER 42

I Have Learned

Based on what I've learned, I came up with a list of objectives or targets that people can set themselves to achieve mental, physical, and spiritual improvement. I believe they are meaningful because they give everyone a tangible focus in their lives.

The aim is not to set ourselves formidable challenges and risk falling short, as that would only compound our sense of unhappiness. Rather, they are simple tasks that can be undertaken daily and that will eventually form part of our unthinking behaviour.

They are to

Connect—expand your network. Reach out to meet people; the more, the better. Whether as friends, acquaintances, or colleagues, the greater our exposure to new people, the greater our experience and horizons.

Stay active. Keeping fit and working hard make us better and more worthwhile individuals, both physically and mentally. Regular exercise also releases endorphins into your body, which make you feel happier and more ambitious.

Notice—be alert and conscious of what's going on around you. It's good to keep up with world events, but noticing what's happening around us is equally important. People talk about living life to the fullest, and by that, they mean living in the present, enjoying the head of the sun, the twitter of birdsong in the morning, the smells, and the warmth of friends and family. The modern term is "iss," which means not wasting time and energy on regretting what's gone or fretting about what might happen next, but living for today as if there will be no tomorrow.

Donate—We all love giving, whether it's a present to a loved one, a few hours of our time to help others, or even paying a compliment or thanking a stranger for a minor act of kindness like holding open a door. Giving away things or ourselves appeals to our natural sense of generosity and reinforces our conviction that people are essentially good and sociable.

Learn—education is what helps us develop and grow. Without knowledge, we can't develop ideas and opinions or make informed decisions.

Enlighten—communicate what you learn. There is little point in developing knowledge and expanding your mind if you don't share your ideas with others. Progress is about the transfer of empirical data from person to person and from one generation to the next. Our greatest achievements, scientific, artistic, and humanitarian, are based on an accumulation of knowledge that began with the earliest forms of life. When communication stops, life stops.

These are things that children seem to understand. As we get older, it seems we start to do less of them. We stop noticing things around us, we fall into habits, we find comfort in routine, and we become isolated, particularly men.

We stop planning, and our ambition recedes. We have created a world where people sit at a task for seven hours a day in front of a computer. If we were to set out with the intention of designing the worst possible experience for ourselves at work, that would be it.

As children, we are exceptionally hungry for knowledge because our minds haven't yet become jaded and dull. Our minds work at an incredible pace, and they are totally in tune with our environment. Our brains work intuitively, absorbing knowledge unconsciously, which is why we can pick up three or four languages simultaneously, especially around the age of four. All of our senses are in synchronicity: touch, smell, sight, sound, and taste—all feeding raw data about the world into our consciousness, informing us about the world without favour or prejudice.

Then something happens that makes us change. We start to unlearn this natural ability to absorb and process information. We fall into patterns of behaviour taught to us by adults that make us question, reject, fear, and discriminate.

We're told not to touch or pick things up; not to bite off more than we can chew; not to speak, read, or watch certain things; not to move, laugh, or cry. All of these instructions were given to us with the best of intentions.

Our parents want to protect us and for us to learn how to protect ourselves to help us fend for ourselves, to keep us away from danger, and to make our way in the world. But the corollary of such advice is that it starts to chip away at our natural desire to experiment, and we start to close things down.

When we go to school, we enter a whole new culture of binary selection, where the world is presented as a series of choices and things are right or wrong, good or bad, clever or stupid, pass or fail.

For the first time, we're told what we're not good at rather than what we're good at.

I have learned to:

Say Precisely What I Mean—Being direct with people and addressing them in a straightforward manner makes them more likely to trust us, feel respected, and feel safe. This is a necessary condition for developing good interpersonal relationships. It's often tempting to use indirect, vague language—particularly when asking people to do something as a way of sweetening the pill. It's a false economy, which invariably is counter-productive when that person discovers they've been given a false impression of the task at hand. "If you have time, can you take the rubbish out?" or "it would be really helpful if you could work through the weekend" are inexplicit requests suggesting that the person has a choice. The result can be that they end up being admonished for failing to fulfil an unclear command or that you, as their manager, end up doing the work yourself. Far better to tell them "Please take out the trash" and "I need you to work through the weekend".

Ask 'How' as well as 'Why?'—Asking why something has happened or not happened is in itself a form of admonition that focuses on the past, the problem, and who is to blame rather than on a solution. Asking, "Why did you not take the trash out?" or "Why did you not work through the weekend to address the fact that the office waste paper baskets are overflowing and that the important report due to be presented to the board of directors on Tuesday morning hasn't been written?" Better yet, how can we ensure that the waste paper baskets are always empty when we come in on a Monday morning?" and "How can we work together to get the report finished by tomorrow morning?" By making a simple change in our use of language, we make those around us feel that they're helping to solve a problem rather than being embarrassed or chastised for having caused one.

Demonstrate Faith in Other People's Efforts and Abilities—Words spoken in a calm tone of voice that communicate a belief in another person's ability to cooperate and to do good work are more likely to achieve the desired result by making people feel respected and able. Taking time to notice and comment on other people's positive behaviour will improve productivity in the workplace.

Focus on what's important, not on what's irrelevant. Words such as 'respect' and 'responsibility' are useful in establishing a culture of behaviour but are less effective when you want a particular task done. Youngsters below a certain age tend to think in terms of specifics. Rather than asking your children to "be respectful," it's more effective to tell them that "when someone else in the room is speaking, listen carefully and wait for the speaker to finish before responding".

Be Concise and Don't Generalise—Whether at home or at work, issuing a long set of instructions can be confusing. Unfair and demanding requests do little to convey your priorities. It can be hard, especially for children, to follow long sequences of words that contain several unconnected messages. To generalise is to assume that the properties of one person count for all similar people. For example, instead of "blond women are dim," which is insulting and wrong, I tend to hear "all politicians are liars" and "all politicians are in it for themselves," which is profoundly inaccurate. If we want democracy to survive, then we cannot label all politicians as bad.

Be Aware When Saying "Nothing is Better"—The skillful use of silence can be just as powerful as the skillful use of words. Using silence opens a space for others to think, rehearse what they want to say, and often summon the courage to contribute. The benefit of silence is demonstrated most effectively when we ask a group of people a question and pause before taking answers.

Researchers (Swift & Gooding, 1983; Tobin, 1980) have found that when teachers wait for between three and five seconds, more pupils respond and that their answers show a higher level of thought.

Remaining silent in meetings, group discussions, or even when sitting around the dinner table with family allows us to listen to what others have to say and requires us to resist the temptation to jump in and question or challenge others before they have had a proper chance to articulate their point.

A good listener attempts to comprehend a speaker's message before preparing a response.

A NOTE FROM THE AUTHOR

When words like 'inspirational' and 'captivating' come as standard and comparison is made to Martin Luther King's legendary "I Have A Dream" speech, you know you are doing something right.

It is all about impact and results. My speaking performances may attract accolades aplenty, but it is those comments that come years after I have spoken that give me the greatest satisfaction. My purpose is to leave an indelible mark on the audience. I want people to 'think different' and 'do different'. I want to see them leave with an extra spring in their step.

Clients want results, especially in these uncertain times: higher productivity, positive culture change, purposefulness, and high-impact communications—internal as well as external. Audiences want a speaker that doesn't just entertain or inform. They want someone who will inspire, challenge, provoke, and motivate with a few belly laughs thrown in.

Looking back from the vantage point of my 74th year, it was probably in my thirties that I started to gain some genuine insight into the patterns of my behaviour and the influences that had allowed me to be, for so many years, at the mercy of circumstance.

I don't describe myself as having been a victim of circumstance because I don't regard myself as such. I've always been responsible for my own destiny, albeit not always in control of it, and while my past is chequered with perhaps more lows than highs, I have no-one other than myself to blame for those low points.

Accepting responsibility became imperative for me when I recognised that only by doing so could I move forward. I've learned that we all succeed or fail, not because of external influences but because of our actions and decisions. Of course, ideas about success and failure are relative, and it would be unfair to judge everyone, no matter how impoverished or privileged their background, by the same criteria. I believe we all have the potential to be better than we are by doing something positive, which has been my guiding principle for the past forty years.

How then can we ensure that language benefits us as individuals in our personal lives as well as managers and employees in a professional setting?

In my work, I have developed a range of strategies to encourage friends, family members, and colleagues to think positively, to ask open-ended questions that stretch other people's thinking, or to redirect them when their behaviour deviates.

ABOUT THE AUTHOR

One of the UK's most sought-after creative thinkers, author Mike Stevenson, offers an exhilarating, inspiring, and mind-blowing hour as a speaker who gets accolades whenever he opens his mouth. Fearless, charismatic, funny, and hugely inspirational, Mike Stevenson is a must-see and hear speaker who puts exhilaration into business and public services while creating a surge of energy and optimism whenever he takes to the stage.

As a creative writer, Mike writes copy that leaps off the page, inspires customers, and changes fortunes forever. He has transformed reputations and improved countless bottom lines.

Mike's life is filled with remarkable stories and lessons learned the hard way. Expelled at fifteen with no qualifications, he embarked on a downward journey that led to homelessness, depression, drug addiction, and the brink of suicide before turning his life around and founding a multi-million-pound business. Mike spent many months sleeping on the streets of London, then racked up twenty-nine jobs before his twenty-sixth birthday—his CV includes steelworker, wine bottler, hod carrier, hospital orderly, biscuit packer, and community worker. He also enjoyed a stint as a musician and actor.

Mike is an international author, TEDx speaker, and Leadercast speaker with more than 30 years in marketing.

Mike experienced the seamier side of London in the Swinging Sixties before moving to Dublin, where he played guitar and sang on the streets. During this time, he met and made friends with Thin Lizzy's Phil Lynott and Brian Downey.

After being spat on and abused in the lowest places, Mike went on to be lauded in the highest places. Throughout it all, he has retained an unflappable faith in the essential goodness of people and in the strength of the human spirit to prevail against the odds.

You'll find more about Mike on his website:

www.MikeStevenson.net

You can connect with Mike here: mike@thinktastic.co.uk

Printed in Dunstable, United Kingdom